The Money Book

The Money Book

A Survival Strategy for Canadians Under 35

Kevin Cork
The Screaming Capitalist

KEY PORTER  BOOKS

National Library of Canada Cataloguing in Publication Data

Cork, Kevin, 1962–
       The money book : a survival strategy for Canadians under 35

ISBN: 1-55263-404-3

1. Finance, Personal – Canada. I. Title.

HG179.C664 2002   332.024'00971   C2001-901691-3

THE CANADA COUNCIL | LE CONSEIL DES ARTS
FOR THE ARTS | DU CANADA
SINCE 1957 | DEPUIS 1957

ONTARIO ARTS COUNCIL
CONSEIL DES ARTS DE L'ONTARIO

The publisher gratefully acknowledges the support of the Canada Council for the Arts and the Ontario Arts Council for its publishing program.

We acknowledge the financial support of the Government of Canada through the Book Publishing Industry Development Program (BPIDP) for our publishing activities.

Key Porter Books Limited
70 The Esplanade
Toronto, Ontario
Canada M5E 1R2

www.keyporter.com

Design: Peter Maher
Electronic formatting: Jean Lightfoot Peters

Printed and bound in Canada

01 02 03 04 05 6 5 4 3 2 1

This book is dedicated to the **memory** of my loving wife
KAREN CORK 1966–present*

---

* She's not dead yet. I am always just amazed at her **memory**. She
remembers every tiny little PICKY thing I have EVER done.

Acknowledgements

I'd like to thank all the little people for making this book possible: Grumpy, Sneezy, Tinkerbell, Snap, Crackle (not Pop), Lucky the Leprechaun, Tom Thumb, Jiminy Cricket, Thumbelina, Kermit, several Munchkins and a Lilliputian, Mini-Me, the Great Gazoo, Mickey, Joe Pesci, The Brain, Casey and Finnegan.

Ok, actually, I'd like to express my thanks:

First to my wife, Karen Johnson-Diamond (though it's Karen Cork when the bills arrive), for her very realistic "spousal support laughter"; and my son, Griffin, for his insightful commentary about the time I spent on the book—"Dad, you are always on the computer."

To Linda Pruessen my PATIENT and obsessively FOCUSED editor from Key Porter Books who would not let me write in CAPS or **bold**!

To Catherine Urban and the rest of the team at the office for help in gathering material, organizing my life and covering for me when clients called. To my clients for letting me spend 10 years trying out wacky financial theories using (their) real money.

To Steve Kangas and The Fund Library for the chance to develop (and sometimes copy) some of the book's material. To Henry Roberts and the *All-Canadian Money Guide* for basically the same reason. To Ross Gilchrist and Janet Alford for their encouragement and verging-on-tyrannical coaching. To Tim Calibaba and the rest of the TWC Financial Corp for the 5000 copies I'm sure they will buy.

To the writer Dave Barry for his constant inspiration as a

shining example of the "long article that doesn't need to say anything as long as it's odd" writing style to which I aspire.

Of course, I'd also like to thank my father, my sisters and my in-laws for all the subtle hints they dropped over the years about getting a real job. And, finally, I'd like to thank my mother for letting me grow up to be this way.

Table of Contents

Introduction
Enough Stalling

> "If only God would give me a clear sign!
> Like making a large deposit in my name
> at a Swiss bank."
> —*Woody Allen*

AH HA, SKIMMING, ARE YOU? Looking for some advice without having to actually pay for anything, is that it? Good for you. If you want my opinion, you should just steal the book. That way you don't have to go to one of those big-box retailers, buy a very expensive coffee and share your reading space with some misinformed foreign exchange student who thinks she's in a library and actually "shushes" the sales clerks as they walk by.

Now, there's another idea. You could wait and get this book from the library—no charge or embarrassing prison term. Of course, it's going to be so popular that there will be a huge waiting list. Plus, I plan to put deliberate errors in the library version so that you retire actually owing money.

I realize that I'm being flippant. I can do this because I know that only a few of those who should read this book will actually make the effort to buy it, let alone steal it or borrow it from the library. Rather than counting on you, I'm trusting that your well-meaning spouses, frantic parents or meddling relatives will scoop this up and give it to you as a gift.

Anyway, welcome.

Who Should Read This Book?

Who is going to be helped most by this book (aside from clever, strikingly attractive and insightful book reviewers, repeat violent offenders and my relatives)? Unlike most other money books, this one is written specifically for people in their 20s and 30s—or 40s if they spent too long in Europe or on their master's thesis—who are starting out on their financial lives. If you've just finished your education, started your first "real" job, bought your first house, filed for your first divorce or had your first child, this book is for you. It doesn't matter if you're an earnest medical intern, a budding professional panhandler or a slothful first-born son finally, grudgingly, taking over the family business: This book can help.

I wrote the book assuming you know very little about financial matters and you care even less. For some, this book will be too basic, while others will need to read some sections more than once. Regardless, it's still likely to be the funniest thing you've ever read about stock market crashes, income tax penalties, dismemberment and death.

Slapped down by Demographics

Let's start with the basics. If you're under 40, you should know that you are financially hooped. Lots of people over 40 are hooped financially, too, but 20- and 30-year-olds are especially, specifically and systematically hooped. Why? Blame it on the boom.

The boomer population (those born between 1946 and 1964) makes up more than a third of the people living in the United States and Canada. When the boomers were born, a lot of things began to change: Housing development ran rampant as the proud parents struggled to house their new offspring; teachers became scarce as these same kids flooded into schools; interest rates rose and housing prices skyrocketed as the boomers started their own families. Now, this huge chunk of the population—separated at most by 18 years—is moving slowly up the age scale. In the next 10 years, we will see the medical industry grow as more and more boomers struggle to combat the effects of aging. We will also see a huge revamp in how our provincial medical programs work. (And when I say "revamp," do you honestly think I mean they will become better and more comprehensive?)

As the boomers continue to age, many of the things that earlier generations depended on—steadily rising real estate values, government benefits, company pension plans and a never-ending supply of K-tel albums—will begin to unravel. As the demand for houses falls (boomers already have their biggest and last house) and the supply grows (boomers no longer want their big houses, preferring quaint condos/cottages/cabins instead), many analysts expect real estate prices to fall steadily over the next 20 years. (More about this

> If you're under 40, you should know that you are financially hooped. Lots of people over 40 are hooped financially, too, but 20- and 30-year-olds are especially, specifically and systematically hooped.

later when I harangue you about buying a house.) Then, as the boomers move through retirement, they are going to scrub the government and private pension plans clean. As in cupboards. And bare.

CASE STUDY: THE CANADA PENSION PLAN

Pleeease. I know, this is supposed to be the government's cornerstone of retirement income, but did you really think it was for you? How... quaint. If you haven't figured this out yet, the money you are currently paying into the Canada Pension Plan (CPP) is not for your retirement. Under the existing system, current workers support current retirees. This system worked perfectly in the late 50s and 60s (when the plan was created) because:

- There were lots of workers—approximately a dozen for each retiree.
- Each worker contributed to the CPP for approximately 45 years before retiring. Once retired, they collected for only a few years before dying and conveniently taking themselves out of the system.

This fortunate state of affairs led to a huge excess of dough inside the plan. So the government did what all governments are required to do with a huge excess of dough: They wasted it. First, they started enriching the payouts, adding things like the disability program. And when that didn't completely sop up the excess, they loaned the rest out to the provinces at low, low rates, never imagining there would come a day when they might need it back.

Then two very bad things started to happen:

1. People began to live longer!
2. People began to retire earlier!

Soon, more and more retirees were being supported by fewer and fewer workers. People retired sooner (spending fewer years contributing) and lived longer (drawing more money out), causing the average retirement period to almost triple over the past 40 years.

After only a decade or two of deliberation, the government swiftly made an incisive move: They increased the CPP contribution rate from 1.8% in 1986 to 4.3% in 2001. As for the payout, the basic retirement benefit for a 65-year-old was $486.11 in 1986; in 2001 it was $775. The math whizzes among us will realize that, while contribution costs have almost tripled, payouts haven't even doubled. Slick, huh? Bet you can't wait to start collecting—you'll be rolling in it!

Unfortunately, this ingenious attempt to stave off disaster was too little, too late. A few years ago, the CPP reached a line in the sand: More was paid out than collected. People sat up and took notice, and the government realized that a better solution was needed. Slowly but surely, the feds began to wean the provinces off their low-interest CPP loans, bringing the money back home to invest. And after the first year, the surplus was over $40 billion! (Of course, it started at $50 billion.)

Why does all of this matter? Why am I so pessimistic about the future of the CPP and your ability to rely on it to get you out of post-retirement financial snafus? Because all of the above changes have happened before the baby boomers actually retire! Just imagine the havoc they are going to wreak on the system. Consider this: There are far more boomers (86 million) in North America than Gen-Xers (46 million), and they're living longer and demanding more than the actuaries thought they would. (I'm not saying actuaries are a little slow, but just the other day, one told me that she was beginning to think Boy George was past his prime.) I can't watch!

The only upside is that all of the loot that the boomers have squirrelled away in RRSPs, pensions, real estate, etc., will be passed along to their kids when they finally ascend to the great health club in the sky! Trillions of dollars are expected to change hands! Whoo hoo! Toss this book and go party! But on your way out, remember that as benefits are cut back and people live longer, more and more of that dough is going to be spent on keeping the boomer alive and wheezing. It's also worth keeping in mind that the government has plans for a great portion of that dough. RRSPs, RRIFs and pension assets are all considered to be "cashed out" the day a person dies. So, if there's $500,000 in your aunt's RRSP and she kicks off, her income for this final year is going to be the $22,000 she had from other sources and the $500,000 RRSP. That's a total income of $522,000, which sounds great until you realize that the government will take about 45%.

If you're still trying to digest just how badly you've been screwed by the boomers, you probably won't want to hear that there's another generation—the echo boom—waiting in the wings. Just as the last boomer draws his last Perrier-scented breath 40 years hence, the first echo boomers will be in positions of power, doing their best to focus all government and corporate attention on themselves. And you? You'll once again be left in the shadows.

If you're still trying to digest just how badly you've been screwed by the boomers, you probably won't want to hear that there's another generation—the echo boom—waiting in the wings.

So what's a poor Gen-Xer to do? Hide in the back room watching *Dukes of Hazzard* reruns and daydreaming about Daisy? No, Cousin Luke! It's time to get going!

Quit Dickin' Around!

Given that the deck is stacked so firmly against you, you absolutely need to reach out and take charge of your financial future! Unlike your parents or older relations, you're going to get next to squat. However, you've got an ally; a secret weapon, if you will. You've got time. You are going to outlive the boomers, and—because of this wonderful book on financial planning—you will end up with more dough and more advantages than the fat and sassy 55-year-old at the forefront of the boomer horn of plenty!

Traditionally, the concept of financial planning conjures up an image of a wealthy older couple sitting in uncomfortable chairs listening to a rich fat man in a tailored suit talk sagely about "assets," "risk/reward ratios," "margin accounts" and "options" through clouds of cigar smoke. In this nightmarish vision, financial planning is something done by people whose kids use words like "estate," "coming of age," "Cannes" and "trust fund" while recovering with a Perrier after three gruelling sets of tennis in the Mediterranean heat.

Wrong. Financial planning can't be this way anymore. Even if you *are* more familiar with words like "Club Z," "coupons," "low down payment" and "Do-Not-Pay-Until-the-Next-Decade," you know that the world is changing. These changes are forcing most of us, regardless of age or income bracket, to become more financially self-sufficient. The bottom line? We have to take care of ourselves. Unfortunately, this dawning realization is causing more than just a little anxiety.

But it shouldn't be about anxiety. The point of financial planning is not necessarily to make or save a lot of money. (If you were thinking that, I'm sorry.) The point is to have enough for a good life. Now, you may need a lot of money to have a good life. Thankfully, each person's definition of the "good life" is different, but no one's should involve sewage diving, three cases of Spam from the 1940s or being stressed out about money.

I work as a financial planner (and part-time ear model). The longer I do this—the planning, not the modelling—the more I realize how straightforward the financial planning process could and should be. We all know that there won't likely be a "safety net" in our financial future. We also know that if we hope to continue eating into our 60s, we'd better start socking away as much income as possible into RRSPs, pensions and investments. Unfortunately, there are always a few things that seem to stand in our way—lack of time, too little or too much information, procrastination, the fact that we have no money. These elements usually work together to create some very serious hazards to successful financial planning.

If I can get you to spend half as much time on your finances as you would on buying a house plant, shoes or hemorrhoid medicine, you will do very, very well. But to make this happen, you need to work with your biggest advantage, your ally, that secret weapon I mentioned about five paragraphs ago: time.

I am going to rave about this in Chapter 5, but here's a brief example of what I mean. If, as an unnaturally disciplined (and probably nerdy) 20-year-old, you began investing $200 a month in a retirement saving program (as opposed to, say, *beer*), you'd find yourself with $1.8 million on your 65th birthday. If you didn't start investing that $200 a month until you were 30, however, your retirement nest egg would be approximately $685,000—nearly a third less.

> Anyone who is currently less than 35 and does not have a million saved at retirement won't have a "nice" life; they'll have a "fridge-box under the bridge" life filled with dogfood.

"Yeah, yeah," you're thinking. "What do I need a million dollars for? I thought you said I should just worry about having enough for a nice life." Well, sweetcakes, anyone who is currently less than 35 and does *not* have a million saved at retirement won't have a "nice" life; they'll have a "fridge-box under the bridge" life filled with dogfood—generic dogfood! Picture yourself 30 years from now:

You and your partner are off to see the The Mummy XVII: The Great-Grand-Mummy *with full virtual reality skulljack hard-wiring. You're running late, so you stop to get a couple of McKrills and ToFuFries. The meal costs less than $80, leaving*

*you a couple of $10 coins for the parking meter. Your new car—
a one-year-old ChevroHyundai Scooter—was less than $50,000,
even with the optional Coppertone ultraviolet screening package.
You're lucky to find parking so close, since it's always crowded on
$22 Tuesdays—no one wants to pay the regular $40.*

*You're happy to be getting out of the "assisted living" condo in
Ralph Klein Towers, even though the $1 million price tag was a
great deal. Your CPPP (Canada Partial Pension Plan) pays out
approximately $3,600 a month—just enough to cover the condo
fees—and the RRSP you set up with Kevin Cork (doesn't he live
on the new EdCal space station now?) has to cover the rest.*

Are you getting it? This is what life is going to cost you
in the next 30 years if inflation stays at the same rate as it
has for the past 30 years (approximately 6%).

The point of this book is to help you smoothly and
painlessly accumulate a pile of loot large enough to handle these types of costs and still keep growing. But you
have to start now.

How to Use This Book

In my opinion, you'll get the most—and most concrete—use
out of this book by thinking of it as a tool. Or a weapon, if
you prefer. Take it into the bank and try this:

"Look!" (slamming book down on banker's desk for
emphasis, scattering papers, etc.) *"I simply MUST have my
line of credit increased/loan extended/mortgage payments
reduced because there are things I have to buy! Don't you understand?"* (Hint: If you decide to use this approach, get the
hardcover for greater effect.)

For the pacifists in the audience, the book is laid out like this: I break things down into easily read and clearly defined chapters with the idea that you will read one chapter, become excited and resolved, and go out and fix that part of your financial life. You can then come back—eager, drooling—and read another chapter. As you make your way through the book, you'll learn:

- how to love a banker
- why budgeting sucks
- how to freebase on credit
- investing tricks for the criminally indolent

To make this whole process more personally relevant, I've created a few Synthetic Imperfect Money Savers (SIMS) to help you relate the impressive yet unintelligible facts I have spouted to a "simulated" real life. Slick, huh? The SIMS are:

Fred and Wilma: A recently married couple (he's 32, she's 29). They are saving for a house, currently living in an apartment and both working. He's a crane operator at a gravel pit and she is a part-time dental hygienist with a pretty small waist.

Rhoda: She's 26, single and works as a rabbit mechanic for a local greyhound racetrack. She has been working for three years, is thinking about buying a condo and is developing a gambling addiction.

Cherry: Is 31, recently divorced, the mother of three-year-old Chance, and finishing a journalism degree. She has spurned a "gopher" job at a big paper and is now writing and editing an environmental group's newsletter and website on a part-time basis. She also waitresses at a coffeehouse.

That's it. Enough stalling. It's time to get going. Stick with me—this will hardly hurt at all.

1 Money People
Your New Best Friends

> "I trust no one, not even myself."
>
> —*Joseph Stalin*

GOT A TOOTHACHE? Well, there's no sense spending good money on a dentist when all you need is a filling. Probe your tooth with your tongue to find the sore spot, grab a shot of whisky, have Cousin Eunice tie you into a solid recliner, fire up the ol' Black & Decker two-speed reversible and bore a quick hole in the enamel. Then, working with a shaving mirror and one of those light bulbs in a cage that you hang from an open car hood, shove some solder into the cavity and tamp it down with a fork. Theeeere...that'll do ya!

Still wondering why most of us bother to spend valuable time and money on real dentists? (Did you honestly think it was because of the little clip-on bibs, the overly cheery staff and the cheap toothbrush giveaways?) We go because it's easier and simpler and faster than learning how to be dentists ourselves. It's even easier and simpler and faster than reading *Do-It-Yourself Discount Dentistry for Dummies*.

Just as you don't absolutely need to have a dentist, you do

not absolutely have to have a financial advisor, either. Many people enjoy researching analysts' reports and reading tax interpretation bulletins the way other people enjoy collecting stamps or photos of goats dressed up like the cast of *Eight is Enough*. (Actually, Willie Aames, who played little Tommy Bradford, went on to appear in *Charles in Charge* and *Dungeons & Dragons* before finding his true calling in the role of Christian superhero Bibleman. . . . But I digress.) For everyone else, this chapter will offer an overview of the people and places that can help you with various aspects of your money.

The Bank

Ahhhh, the bank. . . . The very word conjures up the archetypal monster corporation—foreclosing on orphanages, auctioning off the farm taken from the lame, widowed wife, cheating the kids out of the profits from their lemonade stand with bank charges. How many small business owners toss and turn through the night, convinced that "the Bank" is on its way, swooping down like some dark reaper to close their business, sell their kids and take back all their pens? Of course, the banks recognize this image problem. That's why they give to charity and spend money on heart-warming, touchy-feely commercials.

Unfortunately, the biggest *real* problem we have with banks springs from our own stupidity. The banks "get away" with high fees and lousy service for a simple reason. *We allow it.* Considering the number of complaints I hear, I was amazed to learn that less than 2% of Canadians have ever switched banks. (This lethargy probably stems from the belief that all banks are essentially the same.)

While we're busy whining, the banks work the Grandfatherly Institution image with a "we have always been here, we will always be here" kind of attitude. And, truly, why not? The banks have a point when they complain of too much regulation. They *should* be able to charge whatever they want for an account; they *should* be able to close branches that are unprofitable. Here's the cold, hard truth: Banks are not here to make money *for* their customers; banks are here to make money *from* them. Banks exist to make money for their shareholders. This is not inherently evil. (Unless you have a problem with the whole capitalist concept, in which case, why are you reading this book, comrade?) This is the reason that every single company in the world exists.

The gremlin in the deposit box is the quasi-monopoly that has developed over the years because of banking regulations. Designed "to protect the consumer," these regulations have all but ended competition in the banking industry—and without competition, the consumer has very few choices. Part of the solution to the whole banking problem is to increase competition. Increased competition in any industry forces companies to innovate, cut prices and offer new services. (Just ask the phone company. Does anyone truly think it offers unlimited calling for $19.95 because it wants to?)

Slowly, this is beginning to happen. Securities firms and dealers have begun to offer chequing accounts to clients, including the use of automated teller machines (ATMs). Credit unions have begun to modernize and organize to offer most, if not all, the services offered by banks. Online, companies such as ING Direct and the Citizens Bank of

Canada offer chequing accounts, mortgages and loans that truly compete with what we see from the Big Six banks. As more and more Canadians get comfortable with online banking, the growth potential for these firms is enormous.

But these changes are going to be largely ornamental until we, as Canadians, change our attitude. That's the other part of the solution to the banking dilemma and, unfortunately, it can't be regulated. We need to learn to see banks as simple "money stores." When we walk into a bank to set up a chequing account, apply for a loan or buy mutual funds, all we're really doing is purchasing a product. Yet we don't complain about shoddy service, high prices or poor quality. When the teller informs us that the fees on our three accounts total $30 a month, we nod obsequiously and meekly walk away. We wouldn't take this from any other retailer (except perhaps a French restaurant), so why do we accept it as the normal course of business for financial stores?

Many of us deal with this situation by ignoring it for as long as possible. This is not a workable solution if you want better control of your finances. The truth is that we all need our banks. Moreover, when a bank is properly approached and sufficiently controlled, it can be an excellent ally in your quest for financial enlightenment.

Your Banker's Head Space

To be fair, the average banker doesn't have it easy. In the massive drive for increased profitability, many branch-level staff have had their annual bonuses cut. This is hard to swallow when the headlines are reporting huge profits. The banker must also contend with irate customers who have seen the same headlines, and thus can't understand why their level of service is falling and their fees are rising. Overriding all of this is the knowledge that the branch must succeed as an individual "profit centre." If the branch fails in this mission, head office will replace it—and all of its banker-employees—with a row of ATMs.

So the average banker these days has less money, unhappier clients and less job security than ever before. No wonder most impound lot attendants are former bankers!

So the average banker these days has less money, unhappier clients and less job security than ever before. No wonder most impound lot attendants are former bankers!

Just like most of the rest of us, bankers work for bosses—and bank bosses are a fairly demanding bunch. Primarily, they are interested in two clearly defined client streams:

- The 3% of Canadians who have over $1 million of investable assets. (These people get comfy leather chairs, decaf lattes and perfect kiss marks on their butts.)
- The 97% of Canadians who will blindly pay $5.95 a month to use an ATM. (These people get a lot of nothing.)

The average banker's day is about bringing in more sales—in the form of assets for mutual funds, mortgage or credit card applications, loans or new accounts. Helping current customers with service problems clearly takes away from this focus on new business.

So my heart almost goes out to the typical bank grunt, toiling thanklessly away at the branches—unloved, unappreciated and underpaid. Then I get my statement.

Meeting Your Banker

Okay, given that you now know that you and the banker are both unhappy, hunted and basically miserable, you should feel a lot better about your first meeting.

Now, as your mother told you, first impressions are important. Try to arrange it so that your first meeting with the banker is not because you defaulted on your credit card payment or need a loan for a whisky still. Your first meeting should simply provide an opportunity to introduce yourself, explain your current situation and review your current accounts. Once you've said all there is to say about the $147 in your savings account, take a moment to explain your job/student status and what you are hoping to do with your life.

Don't worry if the banker doesn't seem to be listening; he's probably slipped into "dormant" mode. You may need to employ one of the following key phrases to reactivate him.

- "I'm still not sure what to do with the $244,000 inheritance I'm going to receive from my great-aunt."
- "My father insisted I come in to see you. Your bank was instrumental in helping him earn his first million back in the 80s."

Once he's blinked a few times and sat up, you can hit him with your pre-prepared list of things you'll need in the coming years. For example:

- a student loan
- a car loan
- a mortgage
- an extension on your overdraft
- a credit card (or a better rate on your current card)
- a decaf latte

You should also make some inquiries about how these things work, the various costs and rates, and what the banker expects or needs. Make it crystal clear that you are merely doing some preliminary shopping. (Like you'd do for *any other product*. Get it?) It's useful to make notes on what is offered. It will help you remember things later on, it will show the banker that you are taking this seriously, and it will suggest that he's going to have to work a little to get your future business. (And despite outward appearances, bankers desperately want your future business.) When you leave, take the banker's card, making sure the number allows you to call him directly. This will help you avoid the Press 1—for hours—electronic phone maze.

Don't be too distressed when your decent, helpful banker gets transferred to a different branch six months into your relationship. The bank wants you to stay loyal to the bank itself, not one of its cogs, uh, employees.

Finally, don't be too distressed when your decent, helpful banker gets transferred to a different branch six months into your relationship. The bank wants you to stay loyal to the bank itself, not one of its cogs, uh, employees. Use your first meeting with the new person as an opportunity to explain how the previous relationship worked. Tell her that, although you were initially tempted to walk across the street, you've decided to stay, based on the strength of that past relationship. She'll likely be incredibly agreeable—losing customers doesn't do a thing for career advancement.

Getting a Loan

A week, a month or a year passes. You find yourself in need of a loan. When you return to the bank to apply for this loan, think of it as if you would a trip to a used-car garage, a flea market or some Eastern bazaar. Haggle, baby!

Remember that there are no set prices and few fixed procedures, only deals and "coming to an understanding." Rhoda, whose father owns several rug stores, grew up to the chime of deals being struck. She knows how to deal with bankers:

S I M S   S T U D Y

(A hot, hot mid-day; thin, reedy music in the background.)
Rhoda: Tony, you know I think well of you, my family has always thought well of you. It shames me to say that I was tempted by the credit union's offer of an identical loan at 2% lower interest than what you're showing me here.
Tony: Aiiyee, my manager is not a well woman. She will be sent straight to her grave if I go to her and tell her I knocked 2% off a loan. Please, Rhoda, think of my family!
Rhoda: *(dramatic sigh)* I hate to think of you out on the street and I do not enjoy the paperwork of transferring accounts. Knock it down 1.5%, waive the legal fee and bump my line of credit up another $5,000 so I can walk out of here with my head held high.
Tony: *(long pause, many different faces, muttering, scratching*

on paper) Okay, okay. You know I have a soft spot for you, but no one must learn of what we have done. I will meet those terms if you swear to secrecy.

Rhoda: Deal! (*signs form*) Now come and see the camel I've bought with your money.

Rhoda's little dialogue illustrates why six different people can go into the bank to get a $25,000 line of credit and come out with six different rates and/or repayment terms. The best weapon you have is the right attitude coupled with an awareness of the alternatives. Of course, you are not going to get everything you want. In fact, it's possible that initially you may not be able to get any kind of loan at all. If this is the case, you need to sit down and work with your banker to determine what they need to qualify you for the mortgage, loan or credit card. Don't be intimidated or adversarial. Even if you are refused, remember that it's only because the banker does not have an accurate sense of your worth. If he's completely uninterested, talk to someone else—at the branch, at the bank or at another bank altogether. If you feel you've been dealt with unfairly, write a letter to the branch manager and ask for a new contact.

With the current proliferation of alternatives to traditional banking, it's safe to say that banks need you more than you need them. Few of us would put up with the "bank treatment" if it were dished out at a gas station, clothing store or supermarket. Banks have done an excellent job of portraying themselves as an entity above other retailers, but their business is exactly the same. Don't forget that.

Financial Planners

I am now going to spend a fair amount of time talking about financial planners—what they are, how to find one and how to use one. I am going to do this not because I am a financial planner (and, as such, happen to think they are among the most interesting people on earth), but because a financial planner can be considered the "doorway" to the Magnificent Manor of Money, the Hall of Haul, the Lobby of Loot. For those of you who have no interest in money matters, sitting down with a financial planner is an excellent way to determine your needs and how they can be handled as expediently as possible.

My Bias

Let me state right now that I am completely biased when it comes to this particular subject, and that critics and reviewers should feel free to dump all over me here. For the record, I am a commission-based Certified Financial Planner (CFP) working in Alberta. Naturally, I am amazed at how wonderful my chosen profession and I are.

If you're sitting there thinking that your dad/brother/ cousin/aunt/fairy godmother can take care of your financial future, you might want to reconsider. Fobbing the planning and organizing chores off on a relative, spouse or imaginary friend is cruel and, more importantly, unreliable. Financial planners study long and hard to make sure they understand the complexities of such matters as investing, retirement projections, tax strategies and estate planning. It is highly unlikely that even your Harvard-educated older brother can first become fully versed in all of these areas and then keep up with the constant changes.

The best analogy I have ever heard (I use it all the time when talking to prospects, and I often listen to what I am saying) is that a financial planner or advisor can be compared to a family doctor. Their job is to point out problem spots, assist where they can and then work with specialists to make sure the job is being done right.

Finding a Decent Financial Planner

I recently received an e-mail from a reluctant do-it-yourselfer worried about taking care of his money properly. He was concerned about having to "sit with my limited knowledge and wonder if I can make more good choices than bad while still trying to work 9 to 5 and raise three children and still have time to take my wife out on a Friday night."

He is not alone. For many, the do-it-yourself option isn't really an option at all. Some don't have the skills or the resources to successfully manage their own money; others have the skills but not the desire. Of course, as daunting and exhausting as it can be to create and maintain a financial strategy, it can be just as hard to find someone to do it for you. If I were looking for an advisor (which I may be one day—never underestimate my laziness), I'd follow this simple four-step program.

Know Thyself

Before sitting down with candidate advisors, it's important to determine what you'd like to get out of the relationship. Are you expecting a full-fledged financial plan that encompasses an investment strategy, a retirement plan and a complete insurance/estate needs analysis, or are you merely looking for a good fund to put $200 into each month?

Now, if you've never been to an advisor, you may not have any idea of what to expect. In my comprehensive yet still surprisingly humble opinion, a couple like Fred and Wilma—who have landed half-decent jobs and now want a couple of kids and a house—need their advisor to help them answer a few key questions:

- How much should we be investing in our RRSP?
- What sort of investments are best for our RRSP?
- How can we save more on income tax?
- Should we set up an RESP for our future kids?
- Can we afford a new car, vacation, renovation?

Rhoda, however, will have different goals. Unlike Fred and Wilma, she's not interested in RESPs. At 26, she's not ready for an extensive retirement program or estate consultation. Her goals are to save on taxes, get a basic retirement plan set up and maybe buy a condo. To get appropriate, personalized service, she needs to be clear about what she wants and what she doesn't want.

To help maximize the effectiveness of the time you spend with your candidates, sit down beforehand and rough out your assets and debts. Assets are things you own that are of some value—like the cash you have in the bank, your 1983 Gremlin, and the first X-Men comic. Debts, on the other hand, are what you owe—like your credit card balance and the loan from your uncle that financed the Gremlin purchase. By the way, your assets minus your debts gives you your net worth. Don't worry if it's negative; this is only the second chapter.

Once you've got a handle on this, make a list of what you'd like to achieve financially over the next year, five years and 25 years. Don't worry at this point about what's achievable or realistic, just make the list. A good advisor will drop subtle hints and ask gentle, leading, empathetic questions to let you know that some of your expectations and goals may be unattainable. (One I have used in my practice with a surprising level of success goes something like this: *"What are you—on DRUGS?"*)

Once you've discussed your financial goals, take some additional time to describe the level of service you'd like. As a rule of thumb, I would say that it's reasonable to expect an annual meeting for checkups and reviews, two statements a year and phone calls as needed. Keep in mind that a 22-year-old investing $200 a month needs less attention—barring extraordinary circumstances—than a 69-year-old with a $6 million business to sell and an island to buy off the coast of West Africa. However, if you are that same 22-year-old and happen to *want* a daily statement, weekly face-to-face meetings and Saturday morning walks for your beloved Bouvier, then ask.

If you are that same 22-year-old and happen to want a daily statement, weekly face-to-face meetings and Saturday morning walks for your beloved Bouvier, then ask.

Identify Possible Suitors

So you're ready to start your search. You know what you want and you know what you need. Now what? Ask around for some recommendations. A good place to start is with friends who happen to be r-r-r-rich (or at least happy). Bankers, lawyers or accountants are also good referral sources, but only if you like and trust them.

Although referrals are the best way to find someone, you

might also consider contacting a planner you hear at a lecture or on the radio. Browsing through newsletters, newspapers and financial websites that feature columns by respected planners can be helpful as well. The key is to get a sense of the planner's credibility before you sit down to chat.

Gather Information

Once you have identified a few possible planners, you can set up some meetings. The planner will probably start by asking you some questions. Come prepared to answer the following:

1. What is your net worth? (Whip out your previously prepared list and slap it on the table.)
2. What do you want to achieve? (Ditto.)

Ideally, you're looking for someone who can listen carefully and then respond by saying: This is the approach we take, this is the process we put clients through, and this is the philosophy we have for investing and financial planning. They should also lay out what they expect from you. Depending on what you're asking them to do, you may need to gather your financial records or answer some more detailed questions.

Now you can turn the tables and ask some questions of your own.

What is your education and experience? Of course, education can mean absolutely nothing. One of the most skilled and sensible financial planners I ever met had only a mutual funds license and 17 years of experience. However, a designation (CFP, CLU, PFP or something similar) does indicate some form of training beyond what's needed to get a fund, insurance or securities license. It also suggests that the planner in question is willing to further his or her education. Always a good sign. Here are some of the most common designations:

- CFP (Certified Financial Planner)—regulated by the Financial Planners Standards Council;
- RFP (Registered Financial Planner)—regulated by the Canadian Association of Financial Planners;
- PFP (Personal Financial Planner)—regulated by the Institute of Canadian Bankers;
- CLU (Chartered Life Underwriter)—regulated by the Canadian Association of Insurance and Financial Advisors;
- ChFC (Chartered Financial Consultant)—regulated by the Canadian Association of Insurance and Financial Advisors;
- CIM (Certified Investment Manager)—regulated by the Canadian Securities Institute; and
- JPNB (Just Plain Nosy Bastard)—regulated by Absolutely No One.

What type of products or services do you offer? The various types of financial planner don't necessarily offer every type of service. Some provide tax preparation, for example, while others will refer that service to an accountant. Some work in the insurance or mutual fund industry on a commission basis, and others derive income solely from charging fees.

Most will offer investment advice in one form or another, and most will also be able to do some sort of retirement planning with you. The full range of financial planning activities would include:

- investment advice (building a portfolio)
- retirement planning (projecting retirement needs)
- insurance and estate planning (how to succeed financially from beyond the grave)
- tax planning and/or preparation (how to pay less)
- budgeting (managing your day-to-day spending)
- fashion tips (in the really comprehensive plan)

Do you work with one firm or many? How are you paid? Finding out how the advisor is paid is essential. A good planner will be forthcoming with this information, but you shouldn't count on it being disclosed voluntarily. Financial advisors are paid in one of four ways:

- *They are salaried employees of an institution.* In this case, the institution is most likely a bank or trust company, and the advisor's bias will be obvious. What will be less obvious is the fact that they may be under some pressure to gather all of your financial business—including your investment accounts, mortgage, car loans, etc.—under their roof. Watch for hints about better rates and services in exchange for more business.
- *They are paid a commission on the sale of financial products.* The majority of advisors make their money from commissions paid by the brokerage industry, the mutual funds industry or the insurance

industry. These advisors do not charge their clients a fee.

- *They are paid a financial planning fee.* This is still a relatively rare option, used primarily by big accounting firms that offer national, standardized services. In these cases, the client pays an initial fee for the development of a financial plan that will be reviewed on an annual or semi-annual basis. For a small percentage, the client can also arrange to have his or her portfolio monitored.
- *They are paid by a combination of the above.* There are a few salaried bank and trust company employees who are also eligible for commissions. Many advisors can also work for either a fee or commission, depending on the client. In these cases, the advisor might charge a fee for the preparation of a financial plan. He can then offer to fully or partially offset that fee if the client agrees to use products for which the advisor can collect a commission.

Despite the fervour I felt in my youthful days as a hotheaded, idealistic independent planner, an advisor who works with a company (such as the Royal Bank, the Investors Group or London Life) can be just as helpful as a so-called "independent." However, it is best that you know about any tied relationship from day one. (Quick hint: If they work at your bank branch, they are most likely employed by the bank.)

A lot of debate about fee-based versus commission-based compensation is going on these days. The fee-based types tend to get all preachy about their "true independence," while commission-based planners question whether fees are even necessary. The key problem with how a commission-based advisor (CBA) is paid is the potential for conflict of interest.

The CBA is, of course, much more likely to recommend an investment product that offers a commission. Furthermore, if a particular product pays a higher commission than a similar product from a competing company, the CBA's supposed temptation will be to offer the former. Given the potential for unethical behaviour, many people feel forced to go to a fee-based planner. Within the industry itself, there have even been calls to convert all planners to fee-based pay systems. But this doesn't solve the ethical dilemma. Let's face it: If you are an evil, stupid or insensitive commission-based planner, you're likely to become an evil, stupid or insensitive fee-based planner.

Despite the fervour I felt in my youthful days as a hot-headed, idealistic independent planner, an advisor who works with a company can be just as helpful as a so-called "independent."

The upshot is that there is no right or wrong when it comes to advisor compensation. It all comes down to trust. If you've done your homework, and your advisor has acted professionally, you'll know about any and all fees. There will be no surprises down the line, and you'll rest easy knowing that he or she is working with your best interests in mind.

What is the process? When financial advisors refer to the planning process, they are talking about The Six Steps. We'll spend some more time on this in Chapter 3, but for now, you should know that The Six Steps are as follows:

1. Gather relevant financial data
2. Identify financial and personal goals and objectives
3. Outline financial problems
4. Provide written recommendations and alternative solutions (The Plan)
5. Implement The Plan
6. Provide periodic review

Even if you can't remember all of the steps, you can still appear very clever and well-read (and thus not to be trifled with) by casually saying something like: *"Naturally, I assume you use THE SIX STEPS in your financial planning process. Can you tell me which of THE SIX STEPS you believe is most important?"* (This works really well if you can talk in CAPITAL LETTERS like you're doing an infomercial for the "Turkey Smoker.")

This should wake them up. If they nod and start talking, they are probably fully aware of The Six Steps. If they chortle and wink, they have also read this section of the book. Simply write out a cheque for $50 and leave.

Let's face it: If you are an evil, stupid or insensitive commission-based planner, you're likely to become an evil, stupid or insensitive fee-based planner.

Trust Your Instincts

As important as all of the above information is, you should also pay attention to what your gut has to say. If there is something that annoys you, walk away—even if that something seems completely irrational (such as the colour of the dress the planner is wearing…especially if he doesn't accessorize properly). Financial planning is a trust business, and if you don't feel at ease with your planner, two lives will be miserable in the end. It is essential to take the time to form a good, solid and forthright relationship.

This is your money and your future—you need someone who will take it as seriously as you do.

On an ongoing basis, you must also be upfront about any concerns or problems. And, yes, feeling troubled over watching your investments drop in value is a valid concern. Although this is probably a temporary problem brought on by shifts in the market, your planner should be prepared to spend time reassuring you. If she dismisses your concerns and fears or gets defensive, get someone else. This is *your* money and *your* future—you need someone who will take it as seriously as you do.

Finally, remember that nothing is forever. Like any other pairing, your relationship with your financial planner can be changed or discarded. There's no doubt that this is a stressful hassle, but it is far better to have some tension now than constant worry forever.

Getting the Most from Your Advisor

If you've bothered to go through all the trouble of actually hiring a financial advisor, then I highly suggest that you get your money's worth. Strictly speaking, none of the things suggested below are an advisor's job, but it can't hurt to ask.

- If you're having problems with your statement, your monthly purchases or your transfers, ask your advisor to investigate.
- If you're buying a car, ask your advisor to look over the lease agreement. These documents are hellishly com-

plex, but if she can puzzle out a universal life policy, she's up to the task.

- Ask your advisor to accompany you when you visit your lawyer, accountant, banker, dentist or dry cleaner. If you trust his advice—and you shouldn't be with him unless you do—then getting his feedback or "second opinion" on other financial matters makes sense.
- If you're having problems with debts and/or credit cards, ask your advisor for advice. At the very least, she should be able to point you to the door, uh, provincial or local credit counselling agency.
- Another very sensitive issue is the matter of marital breakdown, or even potential marital breakdown. This is touchy if both you and your spouse use the advisor, but if you are the only client, feel free to ask about mediators, divorce lawyers and, if these first two fail, discount bagmen.
- A drop in the stock market is probably not your advisor's fault, and he certainly shouldn't be held responsible for not being able to predict the future. However, part of the fee you are paying covers "hand-holding," so don't hesitate to call and ask about what's going on.

The key point here is that too many people are reluctant to impose on anyone except their spouses. You should, however, think of your advisor as a high-priced "money escort" and feel free to ask them for anything. Even if they are unable or unqualified to help, they may have the resources and contacts to send you in the right direction.

Other Money People

Accountants

When Genghis Khan was conquering China, he needed to know how many soldiers were in the Chinese army. He called for his Counter of Tents, a scrawny, soft-spoken little mongrel of a Mongol who was good with numbers. Unfortunately, the Counter of Tents was captured and brought before the Chinese general, who demanded to know who he was. Wanting to appear unimportant and therefore not worth killing, the Counter of Tents said quickly, "Oh, I'm just a counter-of-tents, Lord." The general, not understanding, turned to his officers. "What?" They replied, not fully understanding themselves, "Account-tents?" And thus a new profession was born.

These days, accountants come in three flavours.

- Certified General Accountants (CGA)
- Chartered Accountants (CA)
- Certified Managerial Accountants (CMA)

CGAs and CAs do the bulk of all public accounting—helping individuals and small businesses with their tax and financial problems. CGAs cannot do audits; CAs can, and as a result tend to be snootier and pricier. Neither are interested in bookkeeping, but they will have bookkeepers on contract.

CMAs are involved primarily in corporate accounting and financial management. The only time you will need one is when you . . . okay, I've got one! If you are the president of a major corporation, you will need some around to, uh, do financial things.

Once again, it is best to ask for referrals when you're looking for an accountant. A word of warning: Talking to accountants all afternoon can be gut-wrenching, so if you need to take a break in between to calm down, feel free.

Lawyers

Everyone loves to pick on lawyers, but some of my best friends have known lawyers. Lawyers can be very useful when it comes to helping you draft a will, take a company public, draw up a family trust, find the right fit in gloves, debate tax law in the Supreme Court, explain to a judge just how your son ran over the neighbour's cat, hide video tapes, or explain to Vinnie "Kneecaps" Parmigiana why you're late with this month's "donation."

Lawyers can be very useful when it comes to helping you draft a will, take a company public, draw up a family trust, find the right fit in gloves, or explain to Vinnie "Kneecaps" Parmigiana why you're late with this month's "donation."

S I M S   S T U D Y

After her long, drawn-out divorce, Cherry had had her fill of lawyers and accountants. However, her experience taught her how valuable an advisor the right lawyer can be, and she was worried about Chance's future. She has since had an estate lawyer draw up a will to make sure that her assets are distributed according to her wishes. Though initially intimidated, Cherry was impressed with both her lawyer's knowledge and her ability to explain complex legal issues in a straightforward, non-technical manner.

I am going to *strongly recommend* that you hire a lawyer to prepare your will. Yes, you could buy one of those kits from a stationery store, but those pre-packaged forms greatly increase the chance that your ex-wife's ex-husband's sister's adopted stepkids will end up with your family heirlooms, RRSP assets and complete McDonald's Happy Meal toy collection. (You laugh, but wait till you see what they go for in 2020.)

2 Budgeting
Not Just for Dweebs

> "Money differs from an automobile, a mistress or cancer in being equally important to those who have it and those who don't."
>
> —*John Kenneth Galbraith*

BUDGETING HAS BEEN AROUND since the dawn of time. Picture this:

Scene IV, Part 34
Location: Place of small water with rocks (Drumheller, Alberta)
Time: Dawn of
Cue: Cry of strange bird
Characters: Nbhnnk (a financial advisor with the "MnBnk" investment group); Gck (a middle-aged 12-year-old man whose kids have gone off to find their own women); Delores (11 years old and Gck's spouse of 10 years, Delores represents the next step in the evolutionary chain: She uses vowels)

Nbhnnk sits hunched in the dirt of his clients' cave, the only sound the crunch-crunch of Delores eating mites off Gck's scalp.

Nbhnnk: Ht, GHhhn dswwq. Skrrrrr? (*Okay, you need to not spend all your lizard eggs now. Save some for autumn. Can you do that?*)

Gck: Ghh? (*Autumn? But I may be eaten by then! I want lizard eggs now while I'm still young enough to enjoy them! There are a lot of things I want to get!*)

Nbhnnk: Kszzx hrrs nchhws grt... (*Well, I also wanted to talk to you about the winter. You don't have enough set aside, and I'm worried about your dung portfolio.*)

Delores: I *told* him! *Save* your dung, I said! Would it kill you to spend one less egg, I said. But does he listen? No, he just goes to hang out in the vines with his no-good friends—none of whom managed to get all the way through evolution—screeching at the hot six-year-olds and yelling obscenities at the poor Cro-Magnons down the path.

Gck: Jhhggh Cht! (*Look, I work hard all day, getting game and pounding rocks together! It's a jungle out there, and I just want to have a couple of extra eggs so I can go out with boys and kick back!*)

The concept of budgeting is one of the first things they teach you in financial planning school. This is cruel: It makes students think that future clients will actually *want* to prepare a budget. So when we sit down with our clients, we expect to gather enough information to create a nice little pie chart like this:

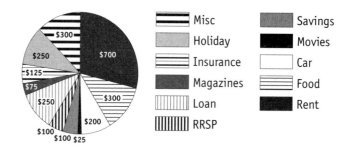

We are also armed with a number of statistics to aid us in our budgeting adventure: The average Canadian spends $270 a month on food, $560 on rent, etc. This information is supposed to help us guide our clients. (*"Holy Macinoly, Daphne, you're almost 17% over the national average in your food spending! Surely you don't need three meals every day!"*)

Statistics aside, a budget is an excellent planning tool for any resource that is limited in quantity—like money, time, oil, peanuts or even bull dung (though there's plenty of that in the investing world). If you're not sure how to create one, don't despair. There are many aids available, including books, seminars and software such as Quicken or MS Money. The latter approach budgeting like a game, with slick 3-D reports and bright vibrant reds to show you how far in debt you are.

However.... After years of trying to both create and live within budgets, I have become a firm unbeliever. I've met with hundreds of clients over the years, and I have come across one—one!—couple that was able to budget precisely and consistently. These two had a set amount of money for food each month, and if that money ran out three days early, they'd live on cereal, potatoes and pickles until they flipped the calendar. It was amazing! (Did I mention that they're divorced now?)

For most people, life is just too short to waste time recording each and every purchase—and forget about projecting spending into the future! This last task is particularly difficult for one simple reason: Most of us spend more money on what we want than on what we need, and it's hard to predict what we're going to want next week, next month or especially next year. No one *needs* to drive a car, eat in a restaurant or buy all the original *Star Wars* toys from 1981, but some of us *want* to. So if you're like 99.9% of the population, who would rather drink battery acid than create and follow a traditional budget, here's the budget plan for you.

The New and Improved Screaming Capitalist Budget

Rather than being forced into a budget that restricts spending, you can use The New and Improved Screaming Capitalist Budget to focus more positively on your future goals. This will allow you to be more relaxed and motivated, and in many ways it will help you to become a better human being (or at least allow you to spend money like a better human being). Let's get Fred and Wilma to help us explain.

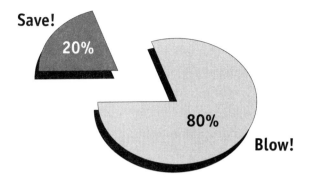

| S | I | M | S | | S | T | U | D | Y |

Wilma learned budgeting from her mother, who learned it from her mother, all the way back to cavewoman times. Wilma shops very carefully, buys bulk on sale and has her coupons organized in a file folder on the fridge. Fred, however, was reluctant to tie himself into any sort of budgetary restraints and hated tracking and recording each dollar he spent. Using The New and Improved Screaming Capitalist Budget as a compromise, Fred and Wilma created a long-term financial plan. They set aside a certain amount each month to cover basic fixed expenses: $1,000 for rent and groceries, $325 for retirement, $150 for car payments and $150 for a trip to Mexico. Now, Fred is free to blow the rest on whatever he wants.

Reading this over, Rhoda thinks: "Okay. It's easy for ol' Cork here to talk about how to meet with money people, how to create a budget, blah blah blah. But I've got a much more basic problem to scream about:

I have no *^%*&^%\$# MONEY!

"So all of this planning and budgeting and investing $250 in an RRSP means *squat* because I don't have an extra $250 to invest in gas for my car, let alone an RRSP!"

That's a fair comment. Many Canadians are in this situation. Each paycheque is completely spent, leaving credit as the only source for extra cash. There's no opportunity to build assets for the future or even to pay down debts. If you are in this situation, your next step is simple: Give this book to someone else.

Just kidding.

Very few people come up to me and say, "Well, we have this extra $250 every month that we just can't seem to spend, so we throw it out."

To be honest, very few people come up to me and say, "Well, we have this extra $250 every month that we just can't seem to spend, so we throw it out." There is *always* going to be something to buy. Our lives—our society—work that way. This problem can be made worse by circumstance. If you are 25 and just out of school, or have recently started a family or moved away from home, there are tons of things you need to buy. There's no getting away from the fact that outfitting a life is expensive.

Despite all of this, it's essential to at least begin the process of saving and investing. If you really don't have extra money, you still have a few options:

- You can wait until later. (This is the most popular option, but also the most problematic over the long term.)
- You can earn more.
- You can learn to spend less.

Earning more is obviously the sweetest option, but it's not a solution in itself. This is because of what I call the "goldfish spending effect." Working at a pet shop while I was in high school, I learned a cool fact: Goldfish will grow as big as their bowls. A small bowl means small goldfish, a big bowl means big goldfish, and a medium bowl means... oh, sorry, you got it? Most of us are goldfish spenders. If we make a lot of money, we spend a lot of money. Very few of us are able to reduce or even maintain our spending in the face of rising income. This was brought home to me when my wife—once a devout garage sale and used-clothing shopper (try saying Va-Lue Vil-Yage with a French accent)—came home with a bunch of bags and announced, "I couldn't decide which one I liked the best, so I bought all of them!" Ah... so.

A larger income won't do you much good by itself. It can help you buy more stuff, but it won't help build assets unless you find a way to spend less than you make. This feat is generally considered a huge inconvenience, something requiring a dramatic change in lifestyle—the quit-your-job-sell-your-car-and-make-a-living-selling-bird-feeders-made-from-margarine-containers crap. If that works for you, excellent. Those of us living in the *real* world can follow some much simpler advice.

Suck It Up!

If you are having a major problem setting money aside for the future, the solution lies in tracking your cash flow, or at least part of it. Now, don't fret. I'm not going to contradict myself and begin preaching the Gospel of Budget. But this *is* a book on managing your money, so it does require you to, well, *manage your money!* The fun part, of course, is that you will manage to save. We will talk later about saving money for big expenses. Here, I want to share some tricks I have seen, created or heard that can help generate the small nickel-and-dime savings that everyone needs to be financially successful. We're going to talk about cash first, so if you're having problems with overspending on credit, take all your credit cards, put them in a bucket of water and put that in the freezer. Impulse credit card spending gets cut way back when it takes 20 minutes to chip the suckers out of the ice.

Saving Strategies for the Fiscally Challenged

I know I've spent several pages ranting about the futility of creating and trying to stick to a budget, but the first part of the budgeting process—officially called a spending analysis in the darkest halls of the secret financial planning cabal that runs the world's money supply (whoops, I wasn't supposed to mention that)—can be very useful. This process requires that you keep a small notebook with you and simply record everything you spend. Most people have no idea where their money goes. In preparing cash flow charts for clients, I add up their incomes, subtract their remembered expenses and then ask what they do with the extra $1,700 they must have each month. I *love* the look they give me—and then each other. If you do the notebook thing, even for just two weeks, you will begin to get a very good idea of where your money goes.

You're not going to do it, are you? Not even for two weeks, right? Come on, admit it. Okay, good. It truly is a pain, and I can give you the results right now anyway. You are going to discover that you spend too much money on:

- restaurants, movies and concerts
- coffee and drinks
- magazines and books
- CDs and videos

These things are the Four Horsemen of Your Personal Financial Apocalypse. CDs specifically are one of the banes of my existence as a financial planner. I know plenty of people who use the fact that old albums are being rereleased (imagine forcing some poor techie to digitally remaster The Captain and Tennille's "Muskrat Love") as an excuse to buy $400 worth of CDs and feel *good* about the $72 dollars they save with their bonus point program. And what is this constant peer pressure to buy videos? We all love certain movies, but are we really going to watch them more than six times? And novels! Don't even talk to me about $50 hardcover novels, or $18.95 for some lame book on financial planning. Go to the library! Read it on the Internet! Borrow it from a friend!

Going out is another big cash killer. Clients who complain about not having $200 for an RRSP contribution are often willing to drop $150 for two concert tickets, $60 for dinner beforehand and $20 for drinks after the show. This makes me insane. Even on a much smaller scale, though, things can add up tremendously—as Rhoda knows only too well.

S I M S S T U D Y

Here is what Rhoda spends—on a monthly basis—buying lunches, novels for the subway and lattes:

Purchase	Expense
Lunches (20 at approximately $8 each)	$160
Novels (three at approximately $12 each)	$35
Decaf soy tall mocha lattes (eight at approximately $4 each)	$32
Magazines (many)	$48
Grand Total	**$275**

But if Rhoda were to borrow her steamy novels from the library, trade magazines with her friends, drink regular coffee and bring her lunch just twice a week, she'd end up like this:

Purchase	Expense
Lunches	$96
Novels	$00
Coffee	$16
Magazines	$24
Grand Total	**$136**

Rhoda would save approximately $140 every month. Now, assuming she takes that $140 and actually plops it into investments that earn 10% a year, she will build up a retirement fund of approximately $466,000. That's almost a half a million dollars for what amounts to some very small lifestyle changes. See how it works? Small savings really can add up!

This "small savings" strategy won't work unless the savings actually *do* add up. In our house, we have a Love Jar (really just a large, unglamorous pickle jar). If we were planning on going out for dinner and a movie but ended up being too tired, we take the $80 we would have spent and plop it into the jar. We even use the jar if we were going to spend $2.99 renting a video but watched a movie on television instead. Once every couple of months, we transfer the contents of the jar to a savings account. When enough "spare change" has accumulated, the money is added to one of our investment accounts, turning small savings into big investments! This one strategy can take care of your savings needs, but you need to *save that money immediately* or it will disappear.

If you have $100 in your pocket, you are much more likely to stop for a beer and a paper than if you have no money in your pocket.

The beauty of the Love Jar strategy lies in its simplicity. It's easy to do, and because it's easy to do, it's more likely to become a habit over time. Once you're in the habit of cutting back a little and keeping a better handle on your cash, another trick is to carry around less cash each day. If you have $100 in your pocket, you are much more likely to stop for a beer and a paper than if you have no money in your pocket.

Here are a few other effective saving strategies:

Payments for Your Future

This is one of the easiest and handiest ways to save money. If you are currently making any kind of payment on a monthly basis (think car, student loan or furniture), set up a new savings account that will continue to withdraw the same amount immediately after the current debt is paid off. If you managed to live without this money while you were making the payments, you can live without it as you begin to save. If you were really struggling, give yourself a break: If your car payment was $275 a month, try putting $250 (or even $200) into an RRSP. Now you're building your investments *and* you have some extra cash. Slick, huh?

Pre-authorize Everything

Forget cloning, the Internet and the fuel cell, one of the *true* wonders of the modern age is the pre-authorized payment system. Whether you use this for RRSP deposits, cable payments or bail, having money flow automatically from your account—without needing to find the bill, write the cheque and mail the envelope—ranks right up there with extra-absorbent paper towels as a modern convenience. You save money because you don't have to pay postage, and you're far less likely to miss a payment (thereby avoiding late-payment and interest fees). If this was a regular problem for you in the past, plop a guesstimate of the saved penalties into your Love Jar.

Review Bank Charges

You can take the electronic advance one step further by looking long and hard at your regular bank charges. Are you getting good value by paying $9.95 a month for your account? Do you really need traveller's cheques and other "perks"? Is there a simpler account that costs less, perhaps nothing? Review the section in Chapter 1 on dealing with your banker and consider some of the cheaper, simpler online alternatives. If this ends up saving you $10 a month, make sure you add it to your Love Jar!

Avoid Junk-Joke Stores

If aliens were to land tomorrow, how could we possibly defend our right to exist if we were caught buying breast-shaped beer glasses, plastic signs saying "I have one nerve left and you're on it," or anything to do with those wild-haired trolls? If you are browsing over lunch (having quickly finished your homemade egg salad sandwich), resist the urge to buy cute stuff from a junk-joke store. Think of the poor Third World child forced to make troll hair in unnaturally bright colours and bank the loonies instead!

Having money flow automatically from your account without needing to find the bill, write the cheque and mail the envelope ranks right up there with extra-absorbent paper towels as a modern convenience.

If, like most of us, you are already saddled with lots of useless junk, answer the questions in this three-part test to determine if you can pitch things.

1. Does the item have any monetary or sentimental value? If not;
2. Have you used the item in the past year? If not;
3. Are you likely to use the item in the coming year? If yes, then...

Toss it anyway! If you've made it through a whole year without taking this thing off the shelf, chances are good that you can live without it. This is not purely economic advice, but for your general peace of mind.

The No-Money Christmas

I'm sure this is the result of my mother-in-law's unsuccessful garage sale, after which she decided to "de-junkify" her house by giving her relatives the leftover stuff. This is how it works: No gifts can be bought for Christmas. Gifts must be used, made, invented, baked or adapted. Last year, I received entries into a dozen different contests, three old records from my mother-in-law's basement, some grocery coupons, and the gloves I left behind the last time I was there.

This may seem strange, but when you think about it, it makes sense. We still have gifts to open, the kids get some real gifts, and there are still drinks, old movies and games—not to mention the turkey dinner. More importantly, the gifts show a lot of thought and represent something more precious than monetary value.

These are just a few examples of how you can save small chunks of money. If you get into the habit of second-guessing every purchase and actually add the unspent cash to the jar, the money will pile up. (Note: If you really are strapped and spent your hard-earned cash on this book, you have my permission to skip this month. But you'd better start next month. I'm not kidding!)

The Curse of Credit

Now that you have a handle on your spare change, it's time for the big leagues—that 300-pound gorilla known as credit. Before you can achieve true financial success by creating and implementing a financial plan, you need to make sure this gorilla is not going to pull the rug out from under your feet. You need him chained up, controlled and hopefully dwindling to just a small monkey on your back.

Don't get me wrong: I love credit cards. I love trading information on my personal buying habits for free air miles, points, credits or whatever. In a very immature way, I am also extremely pleased with the idea that I can have something *now* and not pay until *later*.

And this, my friends, is the core problem with any type of consumer credit—the indescribably delicious but deluded feeling of not actually having to pay. The problem is made worse by the way money flows in this electronic world. You work, money goes into your account, you see it while you're doing your online banking, you buy stuff with a credit or debit card and, sooner or later, the number you see online gets smaller. It's easy to forget that you're trading a part of your very precious life for everything you buy. Think about *that* the next time you buy a dancing pop can!

Admittedly, we would not have very good lives without some form of credit. How many of us would be able to forgo using a mortgage and buy a home outright? Used effectively, credit cards can be an excellent way to control your expenses, defer payment on needed items a little and fund the various emergencies that crop up in life. But for credit to be used effectively, it must be controlled. Using 12 different cards and forgetting who is owed what, how much you have spent and what you've bought isn't "control."

Gone are the days when only the gainfully employed could get a credit card. Credit card issuers now understand that even the unemployed want to buy things. Students, for example, desperately need stuff (drinks, mostly), and if they exhaust their student loans before paying their credit card bills, their parents will often cough up some dough. Banks also understand the advantage of hooking customers as early as possible. They've been reading the latest marketing books and are beginning to fully understand the lifetime value of a client. Thus, more and more students are being offered credit cards during their university or college years; some are even being courted before they finish high school.

How Credit Works

I am always a little shocked and envious when I hear of people not understanding how their credit cards and loans work. I am shocked because I see the use of credit as one of the core pillars that support our way of life. I am envious because I wish I was as good as department stores at finding such financially ignorant customers.

When you receive a credit card from a bank or store, you are being given a loan equal to the spending limit of the card. And, unlike a regular loan from the bank, you can use it—and pay it back—whenever you wish. However, also unlike the loan from the bank, you have little or no choice on the rate of interest you pay.

Credit card interest is a tricky thing. Until the due date noted on your statement, you will not be charged any *initial* interest on the items purchased. If the due date passes

Sample Interest Rates
(as of July 2001)
Bank of Montreal Mastercard 18.5%
Eatons Credit Card 28.8%
CIBC Visa Select (low rate) 10.5%

and you only pay a portion of the bill, however, you are immediately charged the daily interest rate *from the day of the purchase.* You are required to make at least the minimum payment every month; otherwise, your account will be frozen. Most companies prefer not to do this, since it prevents you from ringing up more debt. They will likely call you a few times to remind you about your overdue payment. If you give them the standard "cheque is in the mail" kind of answer, you'll probably get a few days' grace.

One of the most successful marketing ideas in recent years is the system of points and awards for regular shoppers. From Air Miles to Club Z points and GM dollars, almost every kind of business now offers special deals, upgrades or outright gifts for using their loyalty program. Customers love the feeling of getting something for free, but come on, people! Do you really think that the businesses are encouraging you to use these points and get free stuff just because they're nice?

Every time you use one of these plans, you add a new entry into your monstrously comprehensive personal spending file. Stores and airlines want to know who is using their stuff, who is using their competitors' stuff, how often it is bought (at what price, what locations and what time of day), what you are wearing, what you are drinking, when and where you exercise, etc., etc. The more they know about you, the more precisely they can shape their efforts to coax you into buying even more stuff.

Here is a clause from the terms and conditions on the Air Miles Reward Program's website (the bolding is mine):

> *We are committed to protecting your privacy. We collect and use your personal information to: (i) administer the Program, the AIR MILES For Business Program™ and AIR MILES Incentives™, including the management of Collector Accounts to accurately record and update reward mile balances; (ii) process Collector redemptions, including the issuance of Rewards and Certificates; (iii) invoice Collector and Sponsor accounts, as appropriate; (iv) communicate information and offers to Collectors, Sponsors and Suppliers; (v) **understand and analyze Collectors' responses, needs and preferences; (vi) develop, enhance, market and/or provide products and services to meet those needs;** and (vii) enable Collectors to participate in promotions and contests. Ask for our Privacy Commitment for further details. **Collector personal information is considered a Loyalty asset;** if our business is transferred to a new owner, Collector personal information will be given to and considered an asset of the new owner.*

The extra wonderfully ironic thing about this is that I got this information from the Air Miles website and, by doing so, allowed them to track the fact that my computer has gone to look at the terms and conditions page. This is probably a rare occurrence, so now they have me marked as a potential subversive. I won't get my Air Miles newsletter anymore and will never fly free again! *Do you people understand the sacrifices I make for you?*

Understanding Your Credit File

Before a business will grant you a loan, mortgage or any other form of consumer credit (a store credit card or "financing," for example), they must determine whether you can be counted on to pay the money back. Aside from obviously risky customers—like those who ask the sales clerks for a few bucks to get home—there are very few ways a company can quickly decide whether a particular customer is "a good risk," so credit bureaus provide this service.

Credit bureaus are privately owned businesses that charge other businesses a fee for information about your payment history with stores, banks and credit card companies. This includes any information from the "public record" (house sales, bankruptcies, court judgments) that reflects your ability to pay your bills. Your credit file will also contain information you have given companies regarding your name, age, occupation, dependants and spousal information. (It will not keep track of your drinking habits, wine selection skills, known associates, moral behaviour or the breed of dog you prefer.) You have a right to know what is in your file and can see a copy once you show proper identification.

> Your credit file will not keep track of your drinking habits, wine selection skills, known associates, moral behaviour or the breed of dog you prefer.

A credit file is a history, and an accurate history shows both the positive and the negative. So what happens if you, say, defaulted on the loan that you used to buy a half-decent getaway car for your bank robberies but you got caught because you dropped your wallet on the sidewalk on your way out? If it was more than six years ago, don't sweat it. Most derogatory information (bad debts, judgments or collections) is removed from your credit file after six years.

Two quick definitions. Being in *arrears* means you are behind in payments. Stay behind long enough and the creditor will classify you as having *defaulted* on the loan. These are really different shades of the same grey, with one important difference. Being in arrears almost never shows up in your credit file, while defaulting certainly does.

Your Credit Rating

The idea that we all have a single "credit rating" is a popular misconception. This is just not the case. The credit bureau does not rate your file, it simply provides information. Each individual lender has its own standards and policies vis-à-vis the extension of credit. You can imagine that a firm like Paramount Rolls Royce (by appointment only) would have a different rating system than Parole Pete's Tow 'Em in and Drive 'Em out Car Parlour.

If you've never borrowed money, you do *not* have a good credit rating—you have *no* credit rating. Having no credit rating is only marginally better than having a bad one. Unless there is some record of your borrowing money and paying off debts, lenders are completely unable to judge your suitability for a loan. The best way to build a reliable credit rating is to start with small loans and pay them back promptly. Nothing looks better than a credit file indicating that all borrowed amounts were paid back promptly. So, citizen, do your patriotic duty and borrow some money!

If you're new to the credit game, department store credit

EQUIFAX

CONSUMER RELATIONS P.O. BOX 190 STATION JEAN TALON
MONTREAL QUEBEC H1S 2Z2

JANE DOE
10 PLEASANT ST.
TORONTO ONTARIO
M2N 1A2

CONFIDENTIAL INFORMATION
NOT TO BE USED FOR CREDIT PURPOSES
RE: EQUIFAX UNIQUE NUMBER: 3140123054

Dear JANE DOE,

Further to your request, a disclosure of your personal credit file as of **03/27/01** follows:

PERSONAL IDENTIFICATION INFORMATION:

The following personal identification information is currently showing on your credit file.

DATE FILE OPENED: 07/04/92

NAME: Doe, Jane
CURRENT ADDRESS: 10 PLEASANT ST. TORONTO,ON
DATE REPORTED: 12/96
PREVIOUS ADDRESS: 2 AVENUE ST,TORONTO,ON
DATE REPORTED: 12/93
PRIOR ADDRESS: 3 DU BOULEVARD,MONTREAL,PQ
DATE REPORTED: 07/92

BIRTH DATE/AGE: 10/05/1968/33
SOCIAL INSURANCE NUMBER: 123-456-789

OTHER REFERENCE NAMES:
CURRENT EMPLOYMENT: EDITOR
PREVIOUS EMPLOYMENT: TRANSLATOR
PRIOR EMPLOYMENT: CHEF
OTHER INCOME:

SPOUSE'S NAME: JOHN
SPOUSE'S EMPLOYMENT: CHEF

CREDIT INQUIRIES ON YOUR FILE:

Following is a list of Equifax members who have received a copy of your credit file for credit granting or other permissible purposes. Addresses are available by calling Equifax at 1-800-465-7166.

DATE	REQUESTOR NAME	TELEPHONE
03/02/00	CANADA TRUST MTG	(416) 361-8518
02/22/00	TD BANK	(800) 787-7065
01/16/00	BQE NATIONALE	(450) 677-9122

The following inquiries are for your information only and are not displayed to others. They include requests from authorized parties to update their records regarding your existing account with them.

DATE	REQUESTOR NAME	TELEPHONE
03/23/00	SOC ALCOOLS (not displayed)	(514) 873-6281
03/22/00	CANADA TRUST MTG (not displayed)	(416) 361-8518
02/16/00	CMHC SCHL (not displayed)	(888) 463-6454
01/16/00	AMERICAN EXPRESS (not displayed)	(416) 123-4567

CONSUMER INTERVIEWS AND OTHER SERVICES:
You contacted our office in 12/98 to request a review of your credit file.

CREDIT HISTORY AND/OR BANKING INFORMATION:

The following information was reported to us by organizations listed below.
Information is received every 30 days from most credit grantors.

GMAC last reported to us in 01/01 rating your installment account as I1, meaning paid as agreed and up to date. The reported balance of your account was $1000. Your account number: 23456789012345. The account is in the subject's name only. Date account opened: 04/99. Credit limit or highest amount of credit advanced: $4400. **DATE OF LAST ACTIVITY meaning the last payment or transaction made on this account was in** 12/00. Additional comments: auto loan. Monthly payments.

CANADA TRUST MC last reported to us in 01/01 rating your revolving account as R1, meaning paid as agreed and up to date. At the time the reported balance of your account was $285. Your account number: 12345678901234. Date account opened: 06/99. Credit limit or highest amount of credit advanced $2000. **DATE OF LAST ACTIVITY meaning the last payment or transaction made on this account was in 12/00.** **PREVIOUS PAYMENT STATUS:**
30 DAYS: 1 time (s) account previously R2 meaning one payment past due

PUBLIC RECORDS AND OTHER INFORMATION:

The following information was reported to your file on the date indicated.

A COLLECTION was assigned in 10/96 to Commercial Credit by Transamerica Financial in the amount of: $2675. Date reported paid: 07/97. Collection status: PAID. **DATE OF LAST ACTIVITY was in 04/96.** Collection agency reference number: 222222.

A JUDGEMENT was **FILED IN 01/96** in Min Govt Serv. Plaintiff and/or case number: Chrysler Canada 4444. Defendant/other info: joint with Dossier. Amount reported: $7525. Status reported: Satisfied. Date satisfied: 09/97.

A BANKRUPTCY was **FILED IN 08/97** in SC Newmarket. Case number and/or trustee: 5555555 SYNDIC & ASS. Liabilities: $250000.Assets: $8900000.Item classification: individual. Information reported on: The subject only. The item is reported as: DISCHARGED. **DATE SETTLED: 05/98.** Additional comments: absolute discharge from bankruptcy.

THE CONSUMER PROVIDED A PERSONAL STATEMENT to us in 12/98. The statement has been recorded as follows:

RE: BANKRUPTCY, CONSUMER DECLARED BANKRUPTCY DUE TO DIVORCE
This statement is to be removed from the file in: 12/04.

RETENTION PERIOD OF DATA:

Trade reference information is retained in our database for not more than 6 years from the date of last activity reported to us. All inquiries made on your credit file are recorded and retained for a minimum of 3 years and are identified by requestor's name and telephone number.

Public record information is retained in our database for a maximum of 7 years from the date filed, except in the case of multiple bankruptcies which results in retention of bankruptcy information for 14 years from the date of discharge of each bankruptcy. (Exception: P.E.I. Public records: 7 to 10 years, Bankruptcies: 14 years.

These purge rules are in compliance with provincial legislation governing consumer reporting agencies and are used as a standard across Canada. They are intended to reflect an accurate historical and current summary of your credit obligations and payment patterns reported to us.

The attached Reference Update Form is included for your convenience. If you wish to update your file with more current information or to request a change in the information provided above, please complete this form and return it to Equifax Canada. We will ensure that appropriate measures will be applied if corrections are required.

Please be advised that the file you have received is for your information only and may not be used for credit purposes.

Consumer Department

cards are a good place to start. Anyone—alive or dead—can qualify for at least $500, and paying it back is a cakewalk. Just make the minimum payment, pay the 35% interest and have fun. (I read somewhere that Sears used to make more from its credit department than from actual sales. So that's it. After I open my bank—Kev's Bank of Stylish Deposits—I'm going to open a department store—Kev's Stylish Stuff Store and Credit Department.)

On the other hand, if you're all too familiar with the curse of credit, you may want to know what's being said about you. One of the largest and best credit bureaus in the country is Equifax Canada. If you go to their website (see Resources), you can download an application to view your file. (I've included a sample Equifax credit file on pages 67 and 68)

As you can see, the information is quite detailed. There is nowhere to hide, so be careful and watch that facecrime!

Fixing Your File

As you're perusing your credit file, make a note of anything you don't agree with you or any problems you see. The file can be revised, provided the creditor involved agrees. If you can't get the creditor to co-operate, you can still submit a letter explaining your side of the story, and this will be attached to your file. Each credit bureau will have its own procedure for sorting out problems. The key thing to remember is that you have a degree of control over what is reported and how problems are resolved. Don't hesitate to act if needed.

Each credit bureau will have its own procedure for sorting out problems. The key thing to remember is that you have a degree of control over what is reported and how problems are resolved. Don't hesitate to act if needed.

Credit histories can get especially murky in the aftermath of a divorce or split. Just ask Cherry.

S I M S   S T U D Y

When Cherry was married, almost all of the family's credit cards were in her husband's name—although the couple paid off the balances together. After her divorce, Cherry was refused a small line of credit because of her low income and lack of credit history. She contacted Equifax Canada and requested a copy of her credit file. She explained the problem and told them that she wanted to update her record. Equifax advised her to dig through her old records and find information on:

- accounts in her ex-spouse's name that she had used;
- accounts in her ex-spouse's name where she was also contractually liable for payment (or where "community property" guaranteed payment); and
- accounts that she alone had held in either her maiden or married name.

Cherry was also advised to contact all relevant creditors directly and request that they report the account history in both her own and her ex-spouse's names. Without taking this step, information from her creditors would never find its way into her own file.

Credit Card and Consumer Loan Strategies

- As already mentioned, the best strategy for using any type of credit card is to **pay it off!** No investment in the world can guarantee the same kind of "return" on your money as the interest you save by paying off your cards. For example, if you put $1,000 against your Eatons credit card balance at the start of the year, you will have "earned" more than $280 dollars on that money by the end of December! (Since the card charges 28% interest annually, paying off $1,000 saves you 28% of $1,000, or $280.) In the grand scheme of building net worth, paying off debt contributes to the bottom line just as fast as investment assets.

- If you know you need to make a major purchase, try to **time the purchase** so it comes after your statement for the current month is sent out. Take a minute to look at your credit card statements from the last few months and note the date of the last transactions. Personally speaking, I know that anything I buy after the 24th won't show up until the next statement! For example, my July statement is mailed on June 24, so anything I buy on June 25 won't show up until the August statement. It's a little thing, but it can be an effective budgeting strategy to defer payment for a couple of weeks. Of course, this assumes that you're not carrying a balance on the card. If you do have a balance owing, all purchases become "due" the day they are made—another good reason to pay the card off each month.

- For those of you who carry a balance, it's worth taking an hour or two to **shop around** for a low-rate card. This can be done in one of three ways:
  1. Ask your bank to lower the rate;
  2. Ask your bank for a line of credit instead; or

3. Sign up for one of those low-rate cards the Americans love to offer us.

- Use a single credit card account that offers some sort of loyalty program and **grow your points**. We use our Air Miles credit card extensively, for everything from groceries and trips to paying for car insurance and the cell phone. This is handy because it gets us the most points in the least time, makes our attempts at budgeting easier (since everything is on one bill) and gives all sorts of marketers our spending habits. We now get great junk mail, including those low-rate cards mentioned in the last tip.

- If you ever buy furniture from one of those places that offers no payment until the next decade, **offer cash for a discount**. When they refuse, take the $1,400 you had set aside for that lovely purple pleather chaise lounge and plop it into a term deposit to mature until at least a week before you owe them the money. (If you don't pay them on time, they charge you a hideous rate of interest.) If you've used the furniture for two years at no charge and pay it off on time, you have also managed to earn $80 in saved interest.

- Here's an extra tricky tip: **Juggle the Americans**. This last one's so beautiful it deserves further interpretation. Every couple of weeks, I get a letter from some unknown bank offering me a new MasterCard with an interest rate of something like 5.9% for the first six months. I fill out the application, take the card and then use one of the blank cheques they send me to pay off my line of credit at the bank. The bank gets the cheque, sees that it's from a competitor and calls to offer me the same rate on my line of credit for the same six months. I agree and then either use the new low-rate unknown MasterCard to pay off something else or cancel it (because I now have the same rate at my bank for the same six months). Plus, in a couple of months, my name will show up in their files as a former customer and they will mass-mail me again with an application to reapply. It's now gotten to the point where, if I call my bank and *threaten* to pay off the line of credit, they drop the rate for six months. I know it's all a big game (and my wife has told me repeatedly to "get a life"), but *I love* playing one bank off another. It gives me an immature sense of satisfaction, I can save a few hundred dollars a year, and I get a chance to play mind games with the banker.

I love playing one bank off another. It gives me an immature sense of satisfaction, I can save a few hundred dollars a year, and I get a chance to play mind games with the banker.

As you've probably figured out by now, these tricks will not help you simplify your financial life. They will, however, allow you to squeeze the most juice out of your dollar. You have to decide for yourself whether you're organized or interested enough to do the work.

If you've actually worked through this chapter—creating The New and Improved Screaming Capitalist Budget, getting your cash spending under control and taming your credit card gorillas—you have taken a very big step toward true money management. Consider yourself sanctified and anointed, prepared for that holiest of holies, that Grail of plenty—The Financial Plan! Take a deep breath and turn the page.

3 Financial Planning
The Real Thing, Baby

> "Whoooeeee! Eunice! Rope up your monkeys and batten down your lobes! We're about to do some fiii-nancial plannin'!"
> —*Kevin Cork, Certified Financial Planner*

I WAS GOING TO SAVE THIS DISCUSSION for the last chapter because it is the one thing most likely to throw you—or cause you to throw the book. But there's really only one way to make sure you succeed financially, and that is to have a financial plan. We can fool around with budgets and brokers and RRSPs until the cows come home, but without a proper plan to organize everything, the whole set of activities is too haphazard to work.

The only way to get around doing a financial plan yourself is get someone else to do it for you! In my sweet, innocent opinion, this is the best way to proceed. That being said, this section is still important to read. You can glean all sorts of interesting facts and jot down questions to bring up with your advisor. Plus, I've hidden some 3-D nudie pictures in the text, so read it carefully with your head held at a 57° angle, eyes rolled back as far into your head as possible and both feet held in a severe second position like they teach you in ballet....

The Human Race

A financial plan is a strategy to help you achieve both your short- and long-term financial goals, which can include anything from retirement planning to a much-needed vacation. Despite the fact that a financial plan can help you get what you want, most people dread the thought of setting one up, believing that the process will require hours of preparation, meetings and review. But viewing it as a big thing to get over is a mistake. All of the overwhelming and contradictory information out there can actually be boiled down to three basic principles:

- Spend less than you earn (which you are now doing, right?);
- Put what you save in a separate account (such as an RRSP; more on this later); and
- Get an accurate approximation of how much you're going to need for your goals and what you'll have to do to reach them (a plan; more on this right now).

Whether you're a 19-year-old working at your first job or a 57-year-old nearing retirement, you need a financial plan. You even need one if you're already retired. Just imagine what would happen if your money petered out before you did. So don't whine to me about the hassle, you wimp! Just do it.

Maybe it would be easier if you didn't think of financial planning as a single intense "event," like a six-second drag race. Planning for the financial future is really more of a marathon, or a rally. Let's call it the Rat Race, or, even better, the Human Race. Winning requires the same sort of planning as any other race. You have to know where the finish line is (retirement, for example), and you have to know how far away from it you are right now (your current net worth, age, etc.). Before you set off, you'll want to ensure that you know the history of the track and that you've chosen the right car for the race. You could chose one of several vehicles (GICs, stocks, mutual funds), but you should know that the faster you go, the bumpier the ride will be. (It's also more likely that you'll crash at least once before you arrive.) You should also double-check your safety equipment. (Got enough insurance?)

Once you begin, you have to pace yourself and focus solely on the finish line, not how well or badly you did going around that last corner. Keep concentrating on your strategy and don't get panicky listening to the race announcer (also known as a "news anchor" or "headline"). Make sure that inflation, death, disability, taxes and other road hazards don't throw you off track. If your vehicle is performing poorly, pull into the pit and make some adjustments. If you get lost, consult your map—it will help you cross the finish line safely.

(I just want to take a moment to remind everyone how clever I am. It amazes me how well the car analogy covers all the relevant concepts.)

A map forces you to think about where you are and where you're going, but it can't tell you what conditions will be like during your journey. The government may have ripped up the road (changed the investment rules), forcing you to back up and use a detour (think "offshore" instead of "offroad"). You may even need to change vehicles. This is where too many people get bogged down. They use the same type of car as their parents and wonder why they're falling behind. Or they try to keep up the speed through the rough spots and end up in the ditch. This is why your map needs to be reviewed and updated regularly.

In this Human Race, too many of us coast along until the finish line looms in the distance. Then we have to race along frantically just to keep up. Others never leave the side of the road and end up getting left behind. These folks have to rely on a rusty, backfiring emergency vehicle (government benefits) to rescue them—but this vehicle is getting filled to capacity. More and more of these racers are being asked to leave their baggage (their residences, their lifestyles and their pride) on the side of the road.

This is not news. One of the few things the media has done well is scare people about the future. What *is* news is that creating the proper planning vehicle—complete with an owner's manual and a careful map—can be very simple. One of the reasons I wrote this book (aside from the fame and glory and a funky cheese tray at the launch) was to help keep your "car" moving forward without a lot of swerving and hitting too many speedbumps, potholes or, for that matter, innocent pedestrians. I am also firmly of the belief that the more people I can help make financially independent, the fewer I'll have to pay taxes for when I'm old and crotchety (though still ruggedly handsome). I promise to drop the car analogy now, but, man, it *was* clever, wasn't it?

The Process

The financial planning process is made up of several steps. I've decided not to use the six formal steps I mentioned earlier because they're too bland. I have created my own six steps, however, and they are going to require some work on your part.

1. Find out where you are right now.
2. Find out where you want to be.
3. Create a strategy that you can maintain.
4. Decide what to do first.
5. Start.
6. Review your plan every time you buy a new pair of shoes.

As I describe this process over the following pages, I suggest you take a moment, grab a piece of paper* and work through each step. You don't need to spend too much time on it, just enough to get a sense of what needs to be done. However the plan is created—formally or informally—you need to get it down on paper. That way, when you review, you can see what has (or has not) been accomplished.

After going through the planning process, I also want to touch on a few of the major goals that people have to plan for *before* retirement. The same six-step strategy can be used in these cases as well.

---

* You can probably use your Gordon Pape or Brian Costello books for scrap paper since you won't need them anymore.

Find Out Where You Are Right Now

Before you can figure out what you need to save, you need to find out how close you are to your goal. If, for example, you need $750,000 and you win $1 million in the lottery, you're okay. Skip this chapter and flip directly to the end, where my phone number is listed.

In answering the question of where you are right now, you're going to prepare a Net Worth Statement. Despite the scary capital letters, this is simply a list of the stuff you own less the money you owe. If you can do this in your head in five minutes, you really need this book.

Here are the assets and debts Fred and Wilma included in their net worth statement.

S I M S S T U D Y	
Assets:	
RRSPs	$6,800
Canada savings bonds	$1,200
Fred's pension assets	$2,200
comic books*	$800
bank account balance	$1,700
T-bill mutual fund for down payment	$17,000
Star Trek collector plates	$250
Personal possessions (see sidebar)	$2,000
Total Assets	**$31,950**

---

* Don't dismiss these. I used to until I had a client sell his comic books and come up with $17,000 for a down payment. And my mother made me sell mine at the rate of two for a nickel!

Debts:

Student loan	$13,000
The Brick (they don't have to pay till 2010!)	$1,650
Car loan	$250
Credit cards	$750
Total Debt	**$15,650**

Subtracting Fred and Wilma's total debt from their total assets gives them a current net worth of $16,300. They're in pretty good shape.

Although none of these apply to Fred and Wilma's situation, other debts to be aware of include your mortgage; your kids' mortgages; your credit cards; your spouse's credit cards; your kids' credit cards; your ex-spouses' credit cards; your business partner's credit cards; your ex-business partner's credit cards; your ex-business partner's ex-spouse's credit cards.

Personal Possessions
For the most part, you have to value your possessions as if you were selling the whole works at a garage sale. Think in terms of hundreds (not thousands) of dollars especially if you've been stocking up on breast-shaped beer glasses.

By adding up your assets, subtracting your debts and arriving at your net worth, you have discovered the amount of money you can put toward your various goals. Don't get discouraged if you end up with a negative number (meaning that you owe more than you own). It can take years to build up a positive balance, primarily because there are lots of things you need to pay for early in life. As long as the bottom line slowly gets better year after year, you'll be okay.

Find out Where You Need to Be

Financial plans can differ radically depending on your goals. If you want to send your kid to university, you need to plan for four to seven years of expenses. A boat or a vacation or a down payment on a home is a one-shot deal. If you're trying to build retirement income, than you need to consider (hopefully) 50 years. We plan until death, not just until you retire. (Unless you have to keep working until you die... which is not that funny, actually.)

Since one of their goals *is* retirement income, Fred and Wilma have to figure out how much money they'll need to live on once there are no kids to support, no debts to pay and fewer lunches to buy. The rule of thumb is that you will need approximately 70% of your current income. By the time he retires, Fred expects to be making $50,000 a year. Taking that into account, and using an inflation rate of 4%, here is what he and Wilma will need to retire comfortably:

> If you're trying to build retirement income, than you need to consider (hopefully) 50 years. We plan until death, not just until you retire.

Fred's annual income at retirement	$50,000
Fred's annual retirement income (70% of current income)	$35,000
Fred's annual retirement income (adjusted to take inflation and growth into account)	$94,000

What this all means is that Fred and Wilma need to grow a pot of dough large enough to supply $94,000 a year for all the years they are retired, alive and a burden to their family!

As if that's not bad enough, this amount needs to increase a little each year, because as Neil Young reminds us, "Inflation never sleeps."

To illustrate the point more clearly, consider this: If, at 60, Fred needs $94,000 to buy what $35,000 buys him today, by the time he celebrates his 90th birthday, he will need a whopping $300,000. And that does not represent an increase in the standard of living; it just assumes a 4% rate of inflation. (If you *want* to travel extensively, own a life-sized mahogany carving of a bottlenose dolphin or a condo on the Baja peninsula, you'll probably need more money than you have right now!)

An essential aspect of retirement planning is figuring out how long you're likely to be retired. The best financial plan in the world is not going to help you if you screw things up by living longer than you expect. When advisors do projections for clients, they base them on a life expectancy of 90 years. This may seem excessive now, but 20 years hence we could all have our own vats of replacement organs percolating away in some big-box discount laboratory (perhaps Canadian Tissue, where we'll get "bonus bowel bucks" for paying with cash)! The flip side of this particular coin is the age at which you retire.

> An essential aspect of retirement planning is figuring out how long you're likely to be retired. The best financial plan in the world is not going to help you if you screw things up by living longer than you expect.

S I M S S T U D Y

At the moment, Fred and Wilma's retirement plans are based on Fred working for another 30 years, until he's 62.

RRSP Calculator*

Prepared for: Fred and Wilma		Sep 22, 2001
Prepared by: Kevin		22:12:04

Assumptions

Investment rate:	11.00%
Inflation rate:	3.00%
Years to retirement:	30

Retirement Needs

Income frequency:	Annually	
Income required (today's $):	$35,000.00	Inflated: $84,954.19
Income increases with inflation:	Yes	
Years funds to last:	30	
Savings needed at retirement:	$1,053,758.05	

Retirement Savings

Savings at retirement:	$1,053,758.05	
Current registered assets:	$9,000.00	Inflated: $206,030.67
Net amount required:	$847,727.38	
Deposit frequency:	Monthly	

Deposits increase

    with inflation: No

Deposit amount: $299.53

*   This RRSP Calculator was produced with the assistance of Mackenzie Financial
Corporation. Visit Mackenzie on-line at www.mackenziefinancial.com for a variety
of useful investment calculators and planning tools.

Right now, Fred and Wilma are in pretty good shape. If
they hang on to their RRSP until retirement, they only
need to set aside $299.53 a month (increasing this slightly
to keep up with inflation) to meet their goal. If, however,
they use the $6,800 currently in their RRSP for a down
payment on a house (more on this in Chapter 4), they
need to save $354 a month to keep their retirement
income the same.

Things change dramatically if Fred decides he wants to
retire five years early. Now he needs to save $573 a month
rather than $299 or $354. The amount jumps because
Fred has five *less* years of depositing money and five *more*
years of withdrawing.

Putting all of this information together and figuring
things out will take most of a weekend. *(Not that I care. You
are trying to do this yourself instead of finding someone like me
to help you, so I hope it takes all weekend. I hope you find a mistake and have to spend another whole weekend fixing the
mistake. I hope that when you emerge from your financial cri-
sis, your spouse will have left you because you were always locked
away in the back room muttering about present value and average life expectancy. I hope that you have to do it all over yet again
because you were including your ex-spouse's income in your calculations and now there's no chance of that.)*

Create a Strategy That You Can Maintain

This is another area where people get bogged down. Many go to all the trouble of having a retirement projection created, only to learn that they need to save about $100 more a month than they currently make. In this case, the best solution is to start with something—*anything*—and then explore ways to either cut back your spending or earn more. In the SIMS study above, Fred may decide that he needs to work until he's 62, since he and Wilma can't currently afford a monthly RRSP contribution of $573.

The amount you need to save should not be so onerous that you have no money left for anything else. It is far better to play with the numbers and get started with a small amount, recognizing that you can bump it up later.

Aside from RRSPs, other saving and investment options include your rich great-aunt, GICs, term deposits, Treasury bills, lottery tickets, Canada savings bonds, mutual funds, Russian nesting dolls, stocks, shares, rental property, and that ever-so-popular McDonald's styrofoam hamburger clamshell. *(The ones they don't make any more. My grand-mother has over 200 washed and stacked in her basement. She looked at cigar boxes, projected forward and concluded that these would be the next generation's antiques. She may be wrong, but at least she's diversified.)* We'll look at some of these options more closely in Chapters 4 and 5.

Some people are willing to have no life, live on potatoes and Pez, steal from Goodwill and reuse stamps if it means they can quit working a few years early.

Decide What to Do First

Unless you have unlimited amounts of money (in which case, why are you bothering to plan?), you will have to prioritize your financial goals. This is a value issue. For some people, coming up with a down payment is more important than saving for retirement. For others, retiring at 55 is much more important than having a new car, owning a llama, spending a day at the spa or sending their kids to the Calgary Stampede. Some people are willing to have no life, live on potatoes and Pez, steal from Goodwill and reuse stamps if it means they can quit working a few years early. Personally, I would advise against this. Imagine the irony if you get hit by a bus at 56...or 54. The point is that everyone has to sort out what is important to them.

Planning to travel this year, get married next year and have a kid in three years will get "shuffled" if your girlfriend forgets her birth control for a couple of nights.

You also have to recognize that life will often change your priorities for you. Planning to travel this year, get married next year and have a kid in three years will get "shuffled" if your girlfriend forgets her birth control for a couple of nights.

When creating your list of goals, think in terms of time frames. What do you want to do in the next year? What about five years from now? Time frames need to be considered and factored into your investing strategy. Having your list of goals prioritized also helps on those all-too-rare occasions when extra money crops up. If you know you're on track for your first two financial goals, then spare money can be split—half for a treat and half to start on your third goal.

Start

As Nike, the Greek goddess of victory, told the Spartans, "Just do it." Most of us spend more time and energy "getting ready" to get organized, physically fit or financially successful than we do actually working toward our goals. But time is the one resource we cannot replace. Remember that you will usually make more money by starting small and starting early than by kicking in big chunks later on. Don't fall victim to that common procrastination disorder, the "asoonas"—as in "As soon as we get the kids back to school/get the loan paid off/get a new car, we'll get organized and start saving for the future." Forget the excuses and get going.

Review Your Plan Every Time You Buy a New Pair of Shoes

I'm not suggesting that buying $2,000 shoes should be one of your financial goals. In writing this book, one of my intentions was to encourage readers to spend at least as much time on their financial future as they would shopping for a pair of shoes. It amazes me that people will spend an entire Saturday driving from one store to another comparing prices, discussing features and attempting to sort out the best value on a $150 purchase, but will make investment decisions involving what could become hundreds of thousands of dollars in a few minutes.

On the other hand, no one needs to look at their "shoes" (hint: analogy) every day. Most of us only need to haul them out maybe once a season to make sure they're still in style. Remember:

- Pulling out your financial plan every six months to see if your goals and strategies are still important is essential.
- Pulling out the daily paper to check on changes in your investments is useless.

We are going to have recessions, stock market crashes, boom times, a devalued dollar, steady growth and fluctuating interest rates. There's no reason that the next 100 years should be any different from the last. Tax rules will change, investment strategies will change and your personal situation is also likely to change. To remain helpful and effective, your financial plan needs to change, too.

Common Financial Goals

In this chapter, I've spent a lot of time talking about retirement planning. While this is an incredibly common financial goal, it's only one of many. The six-step planning process outlined above is useful for achieving any financial goal, regardless of time frame or importance. Other goals might be:

- buying a house
- buying a car
- having a kid
- sending that same kid to university
- buying back the comic books your mother made you sell two for a nickel
- buying a vacation property

- completing your Salada tea figurine collection
- travel
- starting a business
- raising bail for your spouse
- leaving your spouse

S I M S   S T U D Y

Cherry has decided that she needs to buy a car before Chance starts school in two years. Here's how the six-step planning process would work.

Find out where you are right now. Cherry has $230 in her savings account and no outstanding debts.

Find out where you need to be. Cherry thinks she will need about $5,000 to get a half-decent car. Taking her $230 into account, she needs to save roughly $4,800 in two years, discounting any interest earned in the savings account (which, at 0.25%, is easy to discount!). This means that she needs to save $200 a month for the next 24 months. She also needs to consider insurance and registration, so she should attempt to save $225.

Create a strategy that you can maintain. If Cherry can save only $175, or even $100 a month, then she should do that and revise her plan, even if it means looking at other options—like delaying the car purchase or buying a cheaper car. She needs to remember that saving $100 a month is better than not saving at all.

Decide what to do first. Cherry's first financial goal is to buy a car.

Start. Cherry needs to call her bank and arrange to have the money transferred automatically from her chequing account to her savings account at a fixed time each month. These "payments to herself" can be increased or decreased as needed, of course.

Review the plan every time you buy a new pair of shoes. Stuff happens. Cherry may be forced to move to another apartment with higher rent. She may inherit a car or meet her own personal Daddy Warbucks. Whenever her circumstances change, Cherry needs to make sure her plan adapts.

After you have worked through this process with each of your financial goals, you can get your New and Improved Screaming Capitalist Budget off the ground. Plug in the amounts that you need to save each month, factor in your expenses, and blow the rest!

4 Saving
Strategies for those with Short Attention Spans

> "Saving is a very fine thing. Especially when your parents have done it for you."
> —*Winston Churchill*

WE'RE COOKING NOW! If you've been following along, you've overcome your fear of bankers, gotten your spending under control, found some monthly income to invest and sorted through all those muddled "one day I'll..." financial thoughts that have been running through your head for years. You've turned them into cold, hard goals that have been written down and planned for in a way that makes you accountable for at least *attempting* to achieve them!

If you paid any attention at all to the last chapter, you know that some financial goals take less time to achieve than others. The next step in working to achieve your prioritized financial goals is to define them as either short- or long term. This is done by estimating how long it will take to realize them. Getting the money together for a down payment may take a couple of years. This is a short-term goal. Getting the money together to replace Prince Jefri as finance minister of Brunei will take considerably more time. This is a long-term goal. As a rule, short-term goals can be achieved via a savings program, while long-term goals require a more detailed investment strategy (more on this in Chapter 5).

Saving—also known as short-term investing—is the first type of investing most of us do. As kids, many of us worked very hard to earn enough coins to pay for a bike, a stereo or a Red Rider Slide Bolt Action BB gun. We'd scrape together bits of money, fill up our piggy banks (mine was actually a stagecoach), and then trot down to the bank to watch the amount slowly grow in a bankbook. When the amount in the book matched the price in the catalogue, we'd pull out the money and race to the store.

As we build our short-term savings accounts today, we need to recall our childhood enthusiasm for the process. (And, yes, I do realize that it's much harder to get gleeful over an emergency fund than a pony.)

Short-Term Investing Vehicles

When saving for short-term financial goals, it's important to remember that the money needs to be invested for both security and liquidity. While a five-year guaranteed investment certificate (GIC) is very secure, it won't do you any good if you need it the day after it's bought. A good ol' savings account—kept separate from your day-to-day chequing account (lead yourself not into temptation; don't link the two on the cash machine)—is a common choice. A premium or Treasury bill (T-bill) account pays a better rate but requires ridiculously large amounts of money to earn the extra 1% or 2% annual return.

Instead of a bank account, I would suggest either a 30- to 90-day term deposit, a Canada savings bond (CSB), a high-interest account from one of the aggressive new online firms or a money market mutual fund (also known as a T-bill fund). All four will earn more interest than a bank account and can be cashed very quickly. If you decide to go with a term deposit or CSB, try buying several small ones; that way, you don't need to cash in the whole amount at any given time. Staggering the purchases so that one term matures every three months is also a good way to increase your liquidity.

Staggering purchases so that one term matures every three months is a good way to increase your liquidity.

S I M S   S T U D Y

One of Rhoda's short-term goals is to save for an upcoming trip. She has decided to use a money market mutual fund as her "savings" account and has asked the bank to link this to her chequing account. Once set up, she can:

- make a deposit by calling the bank and instructing them to withdraw the money from her chequing account;
- process the same transaction online;
- make automated deposits on specified days (Rhoda chooses to deposit $200 on the first of every month); and
- use the telephone or the Internet to transfer money back into her chequing account should she need it.

Rhoda is extremely happy with this arrangement. She has convenient access to her money and she doesn't have to go to the bank to move it around. Furthermore, the fund pays the same interest regardless of her balance. Since transfers are processed quickly, her money also earns interest up until the day it is needed. Given the current state of interest rates, Rhoda's not expecting to make a ton of money. That's okay, though. Her main goal is to keep this money separate from her day-to-day account while still having access. Earning slightly better interest than a savings account is merely a bonus.

Once you've decided on the best investment vehicle for your savings, you can get going. In the following pages, you'll find an examination of four of the most common short-term goals: setting up an emergency fund, buying a car, buying a house and having a kid.

The Emergency Fund

Also known as a "rainy day fund," "cash cushion" or "mad money," an emergency fund is used to provide money for an immediate, unexpected problem. This problem should be serious, like the loss of a job, an accident, an emergency flight or even the breakdown of a needed vehicle (*not* the Sea-Doo).

When I was a child, the little ceramic pot by the phone housed our emergency fund. Inside were several dollars worth of coins, a few dollar bills and even a five! This magic pot—always used but never empty—was the source of the paperboy's income, a last-minute supper ingredient, change for an essential parking meter and, of course, treats from the store. These days, most of us need a little more than spare change in our emergency fund. In fact, an often quoted rule of thumb is two or three months' expenses (not income). Realistically, if you are earning a decent income, you probably won't need this much. If you're relatively secure in your job, have a credit card for emergencies and just can't stand to see too much money sitting there doing nothing, a couple of grand should be sufficient.

If you're just getting started on this goal, I would suggest putting half of your investment money into your emergency fund. When the amount hits your target (say $2,000), you can direct future deposits to other financial goals—such as your down payment or RRSP. If you need to dip into the emergency fund, redirect some of your savings back into it until it reaches the correct amount again.

The only people who *should* stick to the two- to three-month guidelines are the self-employed and small business owners. Not only is your income less secure, you may have big-ticket business items (computers, cappuccino machines or drill presses) that would have to be replaced immediately if they break down. In these cases, it may be appropriate to build an emergency fund inside the company. This is a matter to discuss with your advisor and accountant.

Buying a Car

First, a general word about cars. In financial planning school, we are taught that people should very seriously consider whether they even want a car. From a monetary point of view, buying a new car is a cataclysm. It depreciates by 30% the day of purchase and will drop to half its value in the next three to four years. According to the *Sydney Morning Herald*, operating a car in Britain costs more than food or housing. And for people living in a major city, the cost and hassle of buying and maintaining a car is especially extreme.

However. Buying a car is not really a financial transaction—it's the start of a relationship. Thanks to some stunning marketing efforts by car manufacturers, we become more emotional over our cars than any other consumer product. This "passion" is fostered to a point where the suggestion that a car is simply "transportation" brands one as a Non-Driver; someone who Just Doesn't Understand. If you've succumbed to the marketing machine, and still want to make a half-hearted attempt at minimizing the chaos a car could wreak on your financial well-being, then read on.

> According to the Sydney Morning Herald, operating a car in Britain costs more than food or housing.

Car-Buying Strategies

Given the cost of cars these days, it's unlikely that you'll be able to save the total amount needed. However, anything you can do to increase the amount you put down reduces the amount you need to borrow. The short-term investment strategy outlined above will help you build a deposit. If you are now paying off one car and just happen to be thinking ahead, you can also use the saving strategy mentioned in Chapter 3: Once your existing car is paid off, continue to save an amount equal to your current car payment. Your down payment will accumulate faster than you expect. Here are some other suggestions.

- **Buy a used car.** A car that is two or three years old will still have some of its "major components" warranty and most of the newest safety features. It will be available for at least 30% less than a new car, and if you buy it privately, you won't have to pay GST.
- **Consider last year's model.** If you really want a new car, last year's unsold models are a good way to go. They come with a complete warranty package, and they are costing the dealer money every month just by sitting there. Remind the dealer of this during the bargaining process.
- **Look at your current expenses and debts.** A car loan that takes more than three years to pay off is too big. Choose a cheaper car.
- **Consider leasing.** Leasing is a common purchase method these days, and it does work for people who frequently "turn over" cars. But, generally, if you hold on to a car for more than three years (which I would recommend), leasing simply costs too much.
- **Do your homework.** Researching the kind of car you want can help prevent future problems. Reading independent guides like the *Consumer Reports* and *Lemon-Aid* is a great way to learn about the advantages, dangers and problems with each model, style and year.
- **Know what the dealer paid.** If you are going to buy from a dealership, call the Automobile Protection Association (416-204-1444) and find out what the dealer paid for the car. Never mind the manufacturer's

suggested retail price or all the extra options on the sticker. Never mind the sales manager coming by with a printout that "proves" the price. The association will tell you, down to the penny, what the dealer paid. There is a fee for each quote, but the information is worth its weight in gold. One of my clients instantly reduced the price of her new car from $27,500 to $21,900 just by mentioning that she knew the price the dealer paid and offering him an extra $1,000. I was amazed! If you can save $5,600 just by putting in a few hours of research, you're earning a pretty good tax-free hourly wage! And $5,600 invested over 20 years at 12% interest would grow to ... you get the idea.

Talking to Car Dealers

This is a lot like going to see your banker—it can be stressful or it can be fun. It is, however, more likely to be fun, because unlike a banker (who still has a salary to fall back on), the car dealer desperately needs you to buy a car. He also knows that there are a million different sources out there (again unlike the banker, who knows that there are relatively few places you can get a mortgage).

- **Time your visit.** Drop by the dealership at the end of the month, on a miserable, rainy autumn day. Many salespeople are still ranked on monthly sales, so if they're short of their targets, they may be more open to dealing. The next year's models come out in late summer, so go when the current year's models have been sitting there awhile.
- **Take a notepad** and write everything down, flipping

back through pages to confirm what you've written about features, engines, warranties or whatever else you noticed reading the consumer guides. (Salespeople *hate* notepads.)

- **Shut up.** Don't agree with the salesperson's assessment of the great ride, the hot colour or the spectacular vanity mirrors. Make noncommittal noises or just ignore the babbling. Whoever talks the least "wins."

- **Lowball.** Once you know what the dealer paid for the car, add $500 and make an offer. This will cause problems. If he's willing to let you walk away, the offer is too low. (You can always "reconsider.") If he starts talking, he's interested. Hold firm. Hold firm through the salesperson, the sales manager, the finance manager and the general manager. (You'll hear from all of them as they come to reason with you about costs, shipping, sick kids, whatever.) Respond by mentioning that the "forums on the Net" warned of problems with rusting or braking or something. This will psyche them out by demonstrating the depth of your research.

  > It's very effective to take out your chequebook when making an offer. As you lose patience, put it away, stand up and apologize for wasting their time.

- **Flash your chequebook.** It's very effective to take out your chequebook when making an offer. As you lose patience, put it away, stand up and apologize for wasting their time. If you really want the car, you could offer another 1% of your price; but if you do, prepare to start the whole process again.

- **Beware the "trade-in."** Trading in your old vehicle gives the dealer a whole other opportunity to raise his profits. Sell privately or at least get it appraised separately.

- **Beware the add-ons.** *Never* take the extra warranty, the rust-proofing or the upholstery treatment offered. In fact, if offered, look concerned and ask why the factory treatments aren't enough.

- **Focus on the cost.** Find out what the car costs, not how much the payments are. Use a financial planner or banker to help you double-check that the financing calculations are correct. An arrangement with the bank may be cheaper.

- **Keep some perspective.** Remember that there will always be another car you love. Stay calm and have fun—this is one of your only chances to play serious mind games. And don't have qualms; they started it when they advertised on television (plus, they get day-long seminars on mind mastery).

Auto Insurance Tips

You want auto insurance to be cheaper? Get married! People under 25 have the highest premiums because, statistically, they have the most accidents. But *married people* under 25 see their premiums drop substantially. The insurance company knows that, once you're married, you are unlikely to go out to a bar to have fun—ever again (sigh).

After 25, the amount you use the car affects the premiums, as do more obvious considerations such as the type of car you drive, where you live, how many people you have run over and how many police cruisers you have caused to crash. A few notes on coverage:

- The larger the deductible (the amount *you* pay on any accident—typically $100, $250 or $500), the smaller the premiums. This is because if you have a cracked windshield that cost $499 to repair, you will probably use your insurance to pay for it only if your deductible is $100 or $250. Larger deductibles reduce small claims and therefore cost the insurance companies less.

- Although it's not mandatory, getting extra third-party liability insurance makes sense. It's pretty cheap and gives you the comfort of knowing that if you do hurt someone with your car, you can afford to hurt them more than just a little bit.

  Third-party liability insurance is pretty cheap and gives you the comfort of knowing that if you do hurt someone with your car, you can afford to hurt them more than just a little bit.

- Extra family protection endorsement covers off anything awarded to you that the other driver can't afford. Like third-party liability insurance, this is worth the extra cost.

- If you're driving a 10-year-old Hyundai, you don't need a "Ferrari-style" insurance policy. If you total the car— meaning that the car will cost more to repair than it's worth—your high-cost insurance policy will pay you only what your current car would sell for, which is not likely going to be enough to get a new car.

Of course, different insurance companies will use different terms and conditions, so the best guide here is a reliable agent. Use referrals and word of mouth to check on some options.

An Alternative to Full Car Ownership

If you live in the downtown area of a major city, you may need a car only a few times a month to do a major shopping or take a weekend trip. If so, you may want to consider a sharing arrangement. For example, "People wishing to save money on their transportation costs join a co-op to jointly own vehicles with others. Members pay a small monthly administration fee to cover some of the fixed costs of the car and when they use a car, they pay low fees for it by the hour and by the kilometre." (From the FAQs page on the Co-operative Auto Network's website; see Resources for more information.)

In effect, you are buying a *portion* of a car for use when you need it. This type of arrangement has been around only for a few years, but for the occasional driver it is a very cheap way to have access to a car. The drawbacks (I personally hate sharing anything!) are related primarily to convenience, but more and more Canadians are considering this as an option. Car-sharing groups even exist in oil-loving Calgary. They have to meet in secret, of course, and the city makes them wear scarlet letters, but their numbers are growing.

Buying a House

The decision to buy a house is one of the biggest you will ever make. Even finding a spouse takes less effort, money and commitment. But the house remains one of the key facets of the Canadian dream—which is really just a version of the American dream, with more health care and fewer bars on the windows.

Your first decision is whether you really *want* to buy a

house. Personally, I enjoy my own house immensely. I can practise my bagpipe at 3 a.m., dry chicken carcasses on the clothesline and erect a funky fence out of truck tires painted yellow and purple—and no one can boot me out. (The neighbours need more names on the petition.) However, unlike a lot of homeowners, I have no misconceptions about my house ballooning in value like my parents' house did.

This sad but true fact is the result of the same demolition demographics that are currently gutting our public health care and are about to erode land prices. Most demographers predict that the next 20 years will see a gradual drop in real estate values to the tune of approximately 3% a year. Boomers who still want a house currently own their last. If they do move again, it will be to a recreational property or condominium. If you're under 40 and you're buying one of those mega-houses in a new neighbourhood at the edge of some major city, better think long and hard about who's going to want it when you're done.

If you're currently sitting on the fence, don't be pushed by the thought that paying rent is a colossal waste. While this theory is true to a certain extent, remember that most of your mortgage payment—at least in the early years—is going toward interest. It will actually take you quite a while to start building equity. Here's an illustration of the point:

On a $125,000 mortgage that is amortized over 25 years at 8%, your monthly payment will be $954. Of that, $820 goes to interest, while a whopping $134 begins to pay down the mortgage. After three years of payments on that original $125,000 loan, you have put in $34,000—but you still owe the bank $119,500.

See what I mean? It takes a long time to pay down a mortgage—and for some people, it may not be worth the effort. Your call.

What Can You Afford?

If you do decide to buy a house, your first step should be to determine what you want and what you can afford. Actually, you can skip the "what do you want" crap and go straight to what can you afford. This will determine what you want.

what you can afford matters less than what the bank _thinks_ you can afford.

According to the rough guidelines set out by the Canada Mortgage and Housing Corporation (CMHC), a good rule of thumb is to multiply the family income by 2.5 to get the upper limit of what you can reasonably afford. So if you and your partner earn a combined yearly income of $60,000, you should only consider a dwelling of up to $150,000 in value. Actually, what you can afford matters less than what the bank *thinks* you can afford. They determine this by using two ratios:

- **Gross debt service ratio:** This is 30% of your combined income and represents the amount you should be putting into housing—including heat, property taxes and half of the condo fees, if applicable.
- **Total debt service ratio:** This is the total of all monthly debt payments (including your future mortgage). It should end up being no more than 40% of your gross income.

Once you know what you can afford, you can start shopping. There are two types of house-buying allies who can help you through this process—mortgage brokers and realtors.

Mortgage Brokers and Realtors

I have always used a mortgage broker and I recommend that you do, too. Here's why:

- Mortgage brokers make things easy. The broker faxes you some forms, you fax them back, and the broker goes shopping for your mortgage. This means that you don't have to start calling various banks and trust companies—what a relief.
- Mortgage brokers work with many different institutions—from the big boys to the small places that often offer the best rates.
- Mortgage brokers can advise you about the various mortgage types and offer some informed opinions about choosing the best term and rate.
- Mortgage brokers can help you play one lender off against another.
- Most mortgage brokers won't cost you a penny. This is because they collect a percentage from the institutions they work with. (This bothers some customers, but since my broker was able to offer me a lower rate than the trust company I'd been dealing with for 20 years, I could care less who pays the broker the most.)
- Mortgage brokers keep your information on file. When you apply for another mortgage, you don't need to go through the hassle of starting from scratch. You just need to update the basics.

Overall, a mortgage broker takes a large part of the initial house-buying stress and reduces it to a few faxes and phone calls. Ahhhhhh....

Speaking of stress reduction, realtors—more commonly known as "real estate agents"—can also help enormously. Like all professionals, realtors can be good or really bad, stinky rotten worm-infested apples. Find a Good Apple. The best way is word of mouth (not via the big picture on the billboard), so ask someone who has recently bought or sold a house.

It is possible to go through the whole sell-your-house-and-buy-another-one process without a realtor's help, but then it's also possible to cut your lawn with nail clippers or have fire ants use your tongue for their mating dance. Realtors are involved in the housing market on a day-to-day basis and can use that experience to save you lots of time and lots of hassle—and maybe even lots of money!

> If is possible to go through the whole sell-your-house-and-buy-another-one process without a realtor's help, but then it's also possible to cut your lawn with nail clippers.

It is important to understand that a realtor will receive a percentage of the house's sale price from the seller. This generally means that they are motivated to do their best for you: If the house sells cheap, their cut will obviously be smaller. If you're buying a home from the same realtor that handles your sale, you may be able to catch a break on their commission, since they won't have to split it with another realtor.

Take the time to talk to a couple of realtors before making your choice. Make sure they understand your needs and desires as well as your current situation.

How Mortgages Work... Usually

Mortgages are loans that use the purchased property as collateral. They are set in terms from six months to five years and are amortized over longer periods. Typically, a first mortgage will have an amortization period of 20 to 25 years. The longer the period, the lower the monthly payments. The catch is that the longer the loan is in existence, the more it ends up costing in interest charges. Mortgages can be conventional or insured. If you've borrowed less than 75% of the property value, then you have a conventional mortgage. If you've borrowed a greater percentage—between 76% and 90% (or 95% for first-time home buyers; see below)—then the mortgage must be insured, usually by the Canada Mortgage and Housing Corporation (CMHC). The cost of the insurance is determined by the amount borrowed.

Down Payment (as % of purchase price or appraised value)	Insurance Premium (as % of total mortgage)
5%	3.75%
10%	2.50%
15%	2.00%
20%	1.25%
25%	no premium

If, for example, you put down 5% on a $100,000 mortgage, you would have an insurance fee of $3,750 ($100,000 mortgage x 3.75% premium). Here are a few other mortgage points to remember.

- The interest rate is usually set each term; for example, 7% per year for a five-year term.
- Mortgages can be closed or open. An open mortgage can be paid off at any time but usually charges a higher interest rate for that flexibility. A closed mortgage charges a penalty if the mortgage is paid off before the end of the term.
- Closed mortgages usually allow an annual payment to be applied directly to the principal. Monthly payments may also be "topped up," with the excess going directly to the principal. Most people can benefit from this type of arrangement. Take a mortgage with a long amortization and then bump up payments on this voluntary basis. If you run into financial problems down the road, you can simply drop the payments back to the minimum. Mortgages with shorter amortization periods don't allow this flexibility.
- Look into mortgages that can move with you; otherwise, your current mortgage must be settled (with the penalty) if you move before the term is up.

Paying it down

If you want to know how much biweekly payments can help, check this out. Let's say you have a $150,000 mortgage at 8% amortized over 25 years. With monthly payments of $1,144.82, you'd have the mortgage paid off in 25 years. Switch to biweekly payments of $572, however, and you'll be mortgage-free in 19.9 years. That's almost six years off your mortgage! And don't even talk to me about interest. After five years of payments, the monthly payer would have kicked in $56,892.87 worth of interest; he'd still owe a whopping $138,203.67. Our biweekly friend, though, would have paid $55,456.06 and would owe only another $130,870.66.

Furthermore, your new mortgage will have current (probably higher) interest rates. Thus, portability can be very important if you have a staggeringly low interest rate that you want to keep with you always.

- Paying off a mortgage to the exclusion of other financial goals is not necessarily the best idea, given today's low interest rates (more on this below).
- You could also consider paying your mortgage every two weeks rather than once a month. You will pay off the mortgage much faster because there are two extra payments each year (see sidebar).

Once you have financing arranged, don't blow the whole wad on the cost of the house. You will need a few grand for miscellaneous expenses like land transfer fees, back taxes, legal fees and a brand new set of rattan TV tables. If you are buying a new place, you will also have to pay the 7% GST. You might want to consider buying a one- or two-year-old home in a new neighbourhood. You get the amenities and manage to save $10,000 or more on GST.

Remember also that your life may still change. You may end up moving to take a new job, to finish school or because the court order from your ex-girlfriend "insisted." You may keep your first house only for a year or two, so consider buying smaller to minimize potential short-term losses.

Getting a Down Payment

All of this sounds great, right? Not too bad, huh? So now you take the $25,000 you've saved for the down payment and go buy a house. You *do* have the $25,000 down payment, right? Okay, how much do you have? Oh, really? Is that a financial term?

The best way to get a down payment together is to get someone to give it to you. Failing that, there are several other strategies that will work.

As a rule, a down payment must be at least 10% of the home price. (The first-time home buyer's plan offers an exemption, but we'll talk about that in Chapter 6.) The best way to get a down payment together is to get someone to give it to you. Failing that, there are several other strategies that will work.

- Use your RRSP (more on this in Chapter 6).
- Borrow from the builder.
- Approach your bank about the new promo schemes that lend the full amount of the purchase price (but beware of high interest rates).
- Sell your comic book collection. (Okay, I'm still not over the two-for-a-nickel thing.)
- Save it up a month at a time using the short-term savings strategy outlined in the SIMS study below.

S I M S   S T U D Y

One of the best ways to save for a down payment is the process that Fred and Wilma are currently using.

- They determined roughly what their mortgage would be if they were to buy a house today.
- They decided to save the difference between what that payment would be and their current rent.
- They decided to save an additional $300 a month for utilities and $100 for property taxes.

For example:

Projected Monthly Expenses		Current Monthly Expenses	
$125,000 mortgage	$ 954	Rent (R)	$750
Property taxes	$ 100		
Utilities	$ 300		
		Total current expense	$750
Total projected expenses (TPE)	$1354		
Difference: (TPE–R)	$604		

Each month, Fred and Wilma put $604 into a money market mutual fund toward their down payment. Of course, it's very handy to know if they can manage this kind of saving. If they can't afford it now, how were they expecting to afford it later on?

RRSP Versus Mortgage

There is a hotly contested debate among various financial experts as to whether it is best to take extra money and put it into your RRSP or pay down your mortgage. The answer is pretty straightforward: Put your assets where they will benefit you the most over time. If your RRSP investments average a 10% return over the next 20 years and your mortgage *costs* you 6.9%, you are far better off depositing your extra cash into the RRSP. A few caveats:

- If mortgage rates climb and get closer to 10%, you *would* be better off paying down the mortgage. It's a guaranteed cost and RRSP returns are usually not.
- If you can't stand the idea of debt, then pay down your

mortgage first. Financial planning is designed to generate peace of mind. If you have rationally digested all the information available to you, go with the option that will make you happiest. A good compromise is to maximize your RRSP and plop your tax refund into your mortgage.

- Remember that it's far easier to collapse an RRSP for an emergency (although you will have to pay fees and taxes) than it is to get some of the money paid into your mortgage back.

Having Kids

Let me start by telling you that having kids will screw up your finances in sooo many ways. First, they cost a lot. They need food several times a day—every day! They need clothes and games and boxes of Kleenex, beer and oil filters...it never ends. According to Manitoba Agriculture and Food (I have *no idea* why they track such a thing, but they're the only ones who update their numbers each year), it costs approximately $150,000 to raise a child from birth to age 18—and this assumes that, after 18, the kid won't cost you a cent. It also assumes that you're raising this kid in rural Manitoba, where there are no video arcades, movie theatres or electricity. (Okay, I know that's insulting, but, really, how many rural Manitobans are going to buy this book?) There's also the fact that somebody has to take care of them for *years*. This means that one of you has to stop working or you have to spend thousands on nannies or daycare.

Like the other short-term goals outlined in this chapter,

this one should be planned for ahead of time. One common strategy is to delay having kids until one of you has reached an income plateau that allows the other to quit work and care for the children. Other methods include waiting until certain large debts—tuitions, student loans or the dining room set—have been paid off. An extra-cautious approach involves using one spouse's income solely as a savings source for a period of one or two years. The spouse who is likely to keep working can handle the family's spending (mortgage payments, bills, groceries). The saving spouse's income quickly builds a "child-raising" nest egg that can be used to offset the loss of income.

> It costs approximately $150,000 to raise a child from birth to age 18 and this assumes that, after 18, the kid won't cost you a cent.

Taken together and averaged out, having, raising and then educating a child costs about $300,000. That is money that will never be spent on treats, invested for your retirement or used to outfit the hunting lodge. And there's nothing better that you can spend your money on.

5 Investing
Strategies for the Rest of Your Life

> "Being optimistic after you've got everything you want don't count."
> —*Frank McInney Hubbard*

IN THE LAST CHAPTER, we talked about short-term investing, which I defined as "savings." To maintain the yin/yang balance, we are now going to talk about building your long-term savings and call it "investing." The distinction is really a matter of time—or how long it will be until you need the money. The most important long-term goal is, of course, retirement, and investing for that will and should be a priority for most people. However, many other equally important long-term goals exist. If you have young children, for example, you need to start an investing program for their education. You may have other long-term non-retirement goals such as buying a vacation property or a large Hawaiian outrigger canoe to tour Polynesia (complete with a backup band to play the theme from *Hawaii Five-O* repeatedly). Regardless of the goal itself, any plan that will require more than about 10 years of saving should be considered long-term and the monies invested accordingly.

The Basics

There is no magic secret to investing for the long term. It comes down to a simple formula:

$$Time \times Money \times Rate\ of\ return$$

All three elements are equally important to your long-term investing success.

Time

As I mentioned in the introduction, the earlier you start saving, the better off you'll be. If you were to save $200 every month until you turned 65, and your savings earned a 10% return, here's how much you would end up with if you started at various ages.

Age	Total Savings
20	$1.8 million
25	$1.1 million
30	$685,000
35	$416,000
40	$249,000
50	$80,000

To put it another way, if you wait until you are 35 rather than 25 to start saving, you will have $400,000 rather than $1.1 million—almost two-thirds less! What's more, the 25-year-old has invested only an extra $24,000 over those 10 years! To save the same $1.1 million, the 35-year-old would have to save *$550 a month,* for a total investment of almost $200,000. The 25-year-old's total investment is only $100,000.

Money

Obviously, if you invest $400 rather than $200 a month, you will end up with twice as much money when you retire. That is pretty apparent, but too few people understand how small differences—such as $225 rather than $200 a month—can also add up. For example, if you invest $200 a month for 40 years at 10%, you'll end up with approximately $1.1 million. Add another $25 to your monthly investment, though, and your 40-year investment will earn an extra $140,000!

Rate of Return

The rate of return on your investments is also very, very important. Let's expand on the example from the section on time and look at the 25-year-old who's saving $200 a month. At 10%, he ends up with $1.1 million. If his rate of return drops to 8%, he will accumulate only $648,000—almost 50% less! A 2% difference over 40 years can cause a tremendous reduction in future assets.

Conversely, if he can earn 12% on those same assets, his investments will grow to almost $2 million. This lucky guy hasn't increased his investment amount, he's just taken a little more care with his return.

Investing 101

A large part of the "care" required to earn a superior rate of return involves creating a proper asset allocation. And, while you can invest in a myriad of asset classes, the most common and easily accessible are stocks, bonds and mutual funds.

Stocks

I worry about people. Generally and specifically. I worry about people generally when I see railings on cliffs. If the only thing stopping you from walking off the edge of a cliff is a metal bar, then do the gene pool a favour and climb over. We (as a society) spend so much energy and creative talent on thinking up safeguards that we (as individuals) are usually surprised and angry when something bad happens. ("*Now* look! The bear's eating my leg and *I just got* these shoes. Why didn't they have a sign telling me not to climb into its cage?") If the victim happens to be an American, this anger is usually followed by a single thought: "Can I sue?"

My specific worries revolve around those involved in the stock and bond markets. Unlike the cliff, the markets don't come equipped with trusty reflector signs and "Steep Drop Ahead" warnings. Frustrated by their inability to predict the markets' future, many investors choose to join one of two devout camps—both of which claim to know what lies ahead. The first preaches the Gospel of Fear and Treasury Bills; the second sings a "baby-boom-savers-push-TSE-to-a-billion-by-week's-end" refrain. Unfortunately, the pervasiveness of "up-to-the-minute" market reports only heightens the hysteria. The media often talk about market corrections as though they're catastrophes along the lines of losing both Leslie Neilson and William Shatner at once. But let's be realistic: *Of course* the markets will have corrections. If the Toronto stock exchange's average return is 11%, and it's currently growing at 30%, it will at some point stop growing and fall. That's why 11% is the average!

The media often talk about market corrections as though they're catastrophes along the lines of losing both Leslie Neilson and William Shatner at once.

I love this portion of a much longer quote from a Dean Witter memo dated 1932. In the midst of what must have seemed like the collapse of the Western capitalist system, this man was able to sit down and reason out a future that was both realistic and positive. He wrote: "There are only two alternatives to the future: We are going to have either chaos or recovery. The first assumption is foolish because if chaos comes, NOTHING will maintain value. And since no policy can be based on this impossible event, it must therefore be based on the theory of recovery."

This type of "cold water in the face" thoughtfulness is useful in light of the manic-depressive headlines we see daily in the media. In my own experience, I've seen clients stressed for a variety of reasons. Some watch their friends make 30% or 3,000% on some hotshot stock and start howling for a piece of the action. Others have been running with the bulls and are afraid to keep going in case there's another correction. Sometimes, they're afraid to stop in case there's another boom. When I see these reactions, I know that they, like far too many investors, have forgotten the most *important* fact about stocks and are concentrating on the most *unimportant* fact about stocks. I'll let you in on the secret:

- **The most important fact about stocks:** When you buy a stock, you become a partial owner of the company whose shares you have bought. If the company has popular products or services, is well run and carries a minimal amount of debt, its value will in all likelihood increase. As a partial owner, the value of your portion (your stocks) will also increase. If, on the other hand, the company becomes less valuable, the value of your portion will drop.
- **The most unimportant fact about stocks:** Aside from fluctuations based on a company's value, stock prices will rise and fall on a minute-by-minute basis. These less predictable value shifts occur in response to changes in interest rates, political events, currency fluctuations, weather patterns, economic patterns and the whispers of a Romanian soothsayer/analyst/econo-mist in the wilds of northern Tibet.

You can buy stocks according to their "sector" (financial, natural resources, industrial products) or their size (small-, mid- and large-cap, with "cap" referring to capitalization). Stocks are also grouped according to geographic area. In Canada, most individual investors focus on Canadian large-cap stocks (also called "blue chips") because they are the ones we hear the most about.

Bonds

Bonds are loans. A company, association or government will borrow money at a fixed rate for a fixed term, pay the inter-est on a regular basis and then pay back the principal at the end of the term. If the loan is backed by an asset such as equipment, land or a building, it is known as a bond. Loans without collateral are known as debentures.

A bond's interest rate is determined by both the reputation of the borrower (the province of Alberta would have a higher rate than, say, Todd's Thai Gold Exploration and Steakhouse Company) and prevailing interest rates. Government bonds are considered the most secure, not because of their assets (can you say "deficit"?) but because of their powers of taxation. A bond pays out interest on a regular basis. Its market value can also go up and down, triggering a capital gain or loss. How?

Let's say you buy a $250,000 government of Canada bond that pays 7% for 10 years. If interest rates go up to 8%, your bond will go down in value. It is still paying a guaranteed 7%, and you will certainly get your money back when it matures, but if the new bonds being issued are paying 8%, the market price for your bond has to drop. No one is going to buy a used bond paying less than a shiny new one. In an ideal world, interest rates would go down *after* you buy your bond. That way, everyone in the market will be clamouring for your old, higher-paying bonds. Get it?

Mutual Funds

Lots of people talk about mutual funds without truly understanding what they are. Like stocks and bonds, the core concept is very simple. Even if you see the advantages of using stocks and bonds as the building blocks of your long-term investments, you may not feel comfortable making your own selections. If you are unable to do the proper research personally, the best option is to hire someone to do it for you. Just as the owner of a building can hire a manager to assist in the management of the property, you can hire a professional team of money managers to work on growing your investment in stocks and bonds. This team is paid with a percentage of your portfolio—as the portfolio grows, so does their pay (and vice versa). This is a good arrangement except for one catch: You'd need billions of dollars in investments to ensure that the percentage paid to the managers was small enough that it won't badly damage your return. The easiest way to get a few billion dollars is to pool your money with other people's money. When this pooling happens in a structured, regulated way, it creates a mutual fund.

Over the last few years, many investors have leapt into (and then out of) the mutual fund market without really knowing what they are doing. This leaping in and out is usually caused by corresponding activity in various market indices—with a 12-month lag. The lag occurs when people reading about the one-year return of a fund come to one of two conclusions: This is the only fund in the world and they simply must own it, or this is the absolutely worst thing they could own.

Like stocks, bonds and other investment options, mutual funds are not perfect—and they will never be as "good" as the current hot stock. Even if the fund manager owns some of that hot stock, the returns will be diluted by all the non-hot stocks the manager was idiotic enough to buy. Of course, when that hot stock crashes (as they all will, at least once), the diversity of the fund saves the investors from losing all of their savings in one shot. Mutual funds make sense for other reasons as well.

- **Mutual funds help you diversify.** The fact that we can't predict the future is increasingly beginning to plague my peace of mind. If only we could see a week, or even half an hour, into the future, I'm sure I would be much, much richer. But until I have the time it would take to fully develop the prophecy gene, one of the handiest tools for protecting my assets from loss is diversification. By not putting all of my eggs in one basket, I protect myself from the loss of that basket.

  If only we could see a week, or even half an hour, into the future, I'm sure I would be much, much richer.

  If you were to attempt diversification using individual stocks, you'd need to buy 10 or 20 stocks from each sector. Even if you put just $1,000 into each stock, you'd need at least $10,000 to get even a limited form of diversification. Conversely, most mutual funds can be bought for as little as $25 a month, and they provide you with excellent diversification into anywhere between 50 and 100 companies.

- **Mutual funds are time-effective.** Though online services have made research easier, keeping up with financial news is still a time-consuming proposition. To make smart stock and bond purchases, you need to know what you are looking for, how to find it, how to evaluate it properly and how to discount irrelevant and misleading information.

  Mutual funds effectively allow you to "hire" a large group of financial specialists, managers and analysts who work together to analyze each individual company's history and its management's track record. Some fund managers will actually go out to interview company executives, tour the factory floor and scout out the competition. Others spend more time looking at financial records and the performance of the sector as a whole. Still others focus on the company's stock performance and the markets, actively trading stocks with an eye on the big economic picture.

Mutual funds are always going to be a compromise. But that middle-of-the-road approach that so many stock jockeys dismiss is what allows the average person—who does not see stock-picking as the ultimate hobby—to participate in the long-term growth potential of the market.

A Simple Portfolio

So how badly do you want to begin investing? Are you yawning or frothing at the mouth? If you're burning to start, skip ahead a few pages to Steve Kangas's section on choosing an individual fund. If you could care less—if you just want somewhere to put money so you can buy stuff when you're old—read this section and skip the next. You can go tell your friends that you've studied and sweated and finally decided to invest in a well-diversified, well-allocated and comprehensively back-tested portfolio of diverse asset classes and management styles. Then you can ask them to stop harassing you and turn *Buffy* back on. Ready for the two-step program?

1. Go buy a balanced fund from the bank.
2. Put some money in every month.

Many mutual fund pundits pooh-pooh balanced funds as being too middle-of-the-road—and they are 100% right.

Balanced (or asset allocation) funds are mutual funds that invest in many different asset classes—such as Canadian stocks, bonds and Treasury bills, as well as foreign assets. Balanced funds will make some money during the boom times and drop a little in value when the markets dip, but fund management ensures that its investors are reacting to the market's quickly changing conditions.

Many mutual fund pundits pooh-pooh balanced funds as being too middle-of-the-road—and they are 100% right. Balanced funds are dull, but so what? Over time, they have all gone up! Prior to the mutual fund boom, most people took part in workplace pensions, not realizing that these pension funds were, for all intents and purposes, balanced funds. They had the same conservative outlook, the same diverse mix of assets and even the same type of management team. And guess what? Those people got a pretty good retirement!

S I M S   S T U D Y

If you want to get slightly fancier with your investment choices (only slightly, I promise), you could try a multi-manager asset allocation service. Cherry went into the bank, sat down with Berri the Banker and went through this process to set up her RRSP with one of the bank's fund portfolios. She had to complete a questionnaire that asked questions like, "With your RRSP, would you like to a) make money; b) not make money; or c) all of the above?" The questionnaire analyzed Cherry's answers and tagged her as "loudly and ignorantly aggressive," but Berri talked Cherry into the more conservative balanced growth portfolio—at least to start.

A balanced fund or an asset allocation service are both fine investment vehicles, but neither is very exciting. After you have become more aware of your options, you may want to branch into something more elaborate. If this is the case, feel free to read the next section. If not, keep plunking your dough into the simple fund on a regular basis and go do something else. You'll be fine.

Building a Mutual Fund Portfolio

By Steve Kangas

Before you begin building that investment portfolio that *you and your spouse will be entirely dependent on for 20-plus years of retirement*, remember that you are aiming to build a portfolio of funds that suits both your needs and your situation. Ask yourself the following questions:

- What is my time horizon?
- How much risk can I afford to take?
- How much will I need to invest?

Once you've answered these questions—either on your own or after consulting with your financial advisor, you are ready to begin.

Step 1: Create Your Asset Allocation

This sounds easier than it is. Your asset allocation will be drawn from more than 25 mutual fund categories, including Canadian equity, Canadian large-cap equity, Canadian small- and mid-cap equity, Canadian tactical asset allocation, Canadian balanced, Canadian bond, Canadian short-term bond, Canadian dividend, Canadian mortgage, Canadian money market, US equity, US small- and mid-cap equity, European equity, Asia/Pacific equity, Asia ex-Japan equity, Japanese equity, global equity, international equity, country-specific equity, foreign bond, global balanced and asset allocation, North American equity, Latin American equity, emerging markets equity, real estate, specialty/miscellaneous, science and technology, precious metals, natural resources, and labour-sponsored venture capital.

Funds are tools that can help you achieve your financial goals, and you will select funds from a group of asset classes that is appropriate for you (see sidebar).

By narrowing the field to only the categories (or asset types) that you need, you have pre-screened a universe of almost 4,000 funds. In global equity alone, there are almost

---

What's Appropriate?

For longer-term goals, stocks have historically provided the best return. Furthermore, global stocks have fared better than Canadian stocks, but with increased volatility (meaning that the markets fluctuate more). For shorter-term savings, your best choices are Treasury bill funds (also known as money market funds) or possibly mortgage and short-term bond funds. Be warned, though, that any mutual fund except a money market or Treasury bill fund has the potential to fluctuate in value. For most investment goals, a portfolio of different asset classes is best.

—KC

400 funds to choose from. The Canadian equity category has about 400 as well, while the Canadian bond group boasts 250. Thus, to build any basic portfolio (i.e., a Canadian equity fund, a Canadian bond fund and a global equity fund), you are *still* faced with picking from more than 1,000 funds!

Once you've figured out your priorities and selected the appropriate asset classes, you are ready to choose the individual funds that will assist you in achieving your financial goals.

Step 2: Choose Your Funds

For seven years, I worked as a mutual fund analyst at Midland Walwyn (now Merrill Lynch Canada), so I know a little bit about how the professionals choose their funds. Within the industry, fund performance is ranked in quartiles—the top 25% is considered first quartile, the next 25% second quartile and so on. Funds that perform in the second quartile (above the median) or above, year-in and year-out, are strong candidates for making the "recommended" lists. Analysts will also look at risk, asking themselves if the fund's return was commensurate with the risk taken. Also factoring into the decision are the size of the fund; an examination of its management expense ratio (MER); its taxable distributions and portfolio turnover rate; and its similarity to other funds in the same asset category (which lessens the diversification in a portfolio). When all is said and done, though, it comes down to three key areas:

- **Past performance:** Hot performance figures and five-star ratings are often the first things that catch a prospective investor's eye. Still, these may not be the most reliable indicators of future returns. It is important to ensure that the managers responsible for generating these outstanding past performances are still steering the ship. A fund that has been consistently hot wouldn't seem as appealing if the manager making the stock picks suddenly left.

- **Risk:** Every investment involves risk. Be aware that even funds within the same category can have significantly different levels of risk. Some companies' rating systems take a fund's risk into account by comparing its past monthly returns to those of risk-free Treasury bills. Keep this in mind when you're doing your research.

> Every investment involves risk. Be aware that even funds within the same category can have significantly different levels of risk.

- **The fund manager:** As a big believer in actively managed funds, I think it's critical to know who your money manager is and to assess his or her style and abilities. Admittedly, this can be difficult to do from your home. But, if you follow media articles, glean points from books, listen to what fund analysts are saying and question your advisor, over time you'll get an appreciation for the attributes of your fund manager.

A final word of advice: Don't pick funds out of context. The media does a great job of highlighting funds that have performed very well very recently. Usually, they profile funds that are up spectacularly over the past 12 months. *Be very careful in reading these types of articles.* They can range from run-of-the-mill sensationalism to "investment pornography" (to quote Nick Murray), and they can tantalize you into buying a fund or asset class that's totally inappropriate for your long-term success. Here are a few points to remember when skimming articles on mutual fund investing.

- **Look past the exciting one-year return number** and see how the longer-term figures compare to a peer group (i.e., like-minded funds).
- **Look at the fund's size.** Managers of small funds (less than $50 million) are sometimes able to generate outlandish one-time returns because one or two holdings do terrifically well.
- **Look at third-party references.** Basically, you're looking for a pattern: Lots of attention, lots of favourable analysis, lots of appearances on recommended lists, lots of high ratings from the fund rating services, lots of write-ups in mutual fund buyers' guides. If the fund has made lots of unitholders lots of money over lots of time, you're probably onto something.

If the fund has made lots of unitholders lots of money over lots of time, you're probably on to something.

6 The Registered Plans
RRSPs, RPPs and RESPs Need RSVPs

> "Almost anything is easier to get into than out of."
> —*Allen's Law*

DESPITE RUMOURS TO THE CONTRARY, the government wants to keep everybody happy. It knows that its citizens pay too much in taxes, and it knows that the vast majority are unhappy with that. It also knows that if those unhappy citizens had less taxes to pay, they would spend more on gambling, booze and smokes, thereby creating new jobs for casino operators, brewmasters, Cuban cigar-rollers, marriage counsellors, policemen, doctors, cancer specialists, therapists and paramedics. That is the great government circle of life, but here's the conundrum. How can governments give the public what they need and still keep the income tax as complex as possible? Instead of just reducing the tax rate, they stumbled upon the genius solution of creating registered plans for all our tax-saving needs! Not only do these plans save the public some taxes, they are even more complex than the Canada Customs and Revenue Agency (CCRA) could have imagined in its wildest wet audit-dream!

Despite their complexity, registered plans are almost indispensable in helping you achieve your various long-term financial goals. Of course, they're not *absolutely* necessary. It is possible to use a simple investment account and still achieve financial nirvana. But you should think of the registered plans as a form of cash ecstasy—a rush of dough to help hasten that state of well-funded retirement bliss.

Registered Retirement Savings Plans

Unlike a stock or bond, a Registered Retirement Savings Plan (RRSP) is not a specific investment. It's an umbrella— or a bucket into which you place other investments (GICs, term deposits, stocks, bonds or mutual funds). By placing your investments in an RRSP, you entitle yourself to a tax deduction (it's actually a deferral, but we'll get to that later).

This is how it works. Any money put into an RRSP is deducted from your current income. If you earn $31,000 a year and deposit $2,000 into your RRSP, you can claim that $2,000 against your income. This deduction means that the government will tax you on only $29,000 of your income. If you're in the 40% tax bracket, then 40% of that $2,000—or $800—is money you have already paid in taxes. After you file your return, you will receive a refund of roughly that amount.

While that deduction is very handy, it isn't the plan's biggest benefit. The biggest plus is the fact that the *investments in the plan grow tax-free the whole time they are in there!* Outside an RRSP, investments are subject (at least partially) to taxes that reduce the net return on the assets. Over long periods of time, this can greatly slow down the assets' growth.

There are, of course a couple of downsides to using an RRSP. As mentioned, depositing cash into the plan does not create a pure tax deduction because you will still owe tax on any money you withdraw. If you put that $2,000 into your RRSP and withdraw it a year later, you will probably end up owing the CCRA a cheque for $800. To avoid this situation, money put into an RRSP should be money that you won't need for a long, long time.

Earned Income

Earned income is defined (by me) as money you make for doing something, whether you enjoy it or not. If you just sit around collecting cheques from investments, pensions or RRIFs, this money is not "earned." This is not a value statement, just how the CCRA sees it. By the way, net rental income is "earned."

Another big problem with the RRSP are the limits the government places on contributions. RRSP contributions are limited to 18% of your previous year's earned income (less anything that was put into a pension for you) up to a maximum of $13,500 a year. This may not seem like much of a drawback until you realize that the maximum applies whether you're making $70,000 or $700,000. *(In my world, people who have really lousy jobs would get a bigger deduction than those with cushy jobs—chocolate taster, lottery winnings delivery person or fee-based financial planner. Cushy-jobbers would be able to use only 10% of their income.)* This rule also hampers first-time tax filers. Since the limit is based on your previous year's filed income, people who haven't filed a return have to wait until their second year.

Some people fret over having too much in an RRSP, or that it will reduce the Canada Pension Plan money they collect. In my opinion, fretting over whether you have too

much in an RRSP when you are 20, 30 or even 50 is a tad...
goofy. First, given the statistics on the average Canadian, it's
a good bet that you probably don't. Second, the rules will
eventually change, so take whatever perks you can now and
worry about the changes when they happen. And if you're
still seriously including future government benefits in your
retirement planning, Brer Rabbit, it's time to come out of
the briar patch and reread the "Slapped Down by
Demographics" section of the Introduction.

Of course, if you are convinced to the point of night-
mares that RRSPs are doomed or cursed, then just save
outside the RRSP and relax. For those of you brave enough
to continue, here are a few tips and tricks.

RRSP Tips and Tricks

- You have until the end of the first 60 days of a new
  year to make RRSP deposits for the previous tax year.
  Canadians being what they are, this explains the huge
  rush to deposit money in that last week of February.
  But you'd be far better off if you made your deposits at
  the *beginning* of the year rather than at the end. (By this
  I mean making your RRSP contribution in January of
  2002 *for* 2002 rather than for 2001.) This gets your
  investment working for an extra year, which, over the
  long term, can have significant benefits. If you saved
  $2,000 for 40 years at 10% interest, you'd have more
  than $90,000. By waiting until the end of the year, you
  would have only $82,000. Alternatively, you could con-
  sider monthly purchases. It is easier to invest $200 a
  month than to scrape together $2,400 after Christmas.
- Your RRSP limit is shown on the Notice of Assessment

you receive from the CCRA sometime in May (usually). But, really, who can find that right now? Call the TIPS line found in the blue pages of the white pages (don't even ask about that) under the federal government's "Taxes" section. You'll get an automated service that will ask you some personal questions and then spit out a number. Yes, that really is how much you can put in an RRSP.

- Unused contribution room rolls over to later years. This can be an excellent planning tool. Over the years, your contribution room can grow to be in the tens of thousands, so don't dick around too long or you'll never catch up.

- Your contribution should not be "just enough so I don't have to pay tax." When people say this to me— with totally straight faces—I sit on my hands so I can squelch the urge to slap them. They tell me that they are contributing $5,400 now so they won't owe any tax in April. They conveniently forget they have already paid tax all year! The point is to get some of that back!

- A refund is not like a Monopoly windfall! (Remember the old businessman in Monopoly, slapping his forehead in wondrous joy, his top hat flying off as he receives a cheque for $22? Ahhh, the innocence of youth!) A refund is money that you have *overpaid* the government; money that they have been using—for free—for up to 16 months! Try to never let that happen again.

- The best way to do this is to apply to the CCRA to reduce the income tax deducted at source (usually your place of employment), based on the promise that you will put a predetermined amount into an RRSP by year-end. This will reduce your taxes right now and eliminate the tax refund cheque. Be aware, though, that if you don't put at least that amount into the RRSP, you will have to pay interest on the tax you should have paid but didn't.

Setting up an RRSP

Have you seen the light? Are you ready to take the next step? Setting up an RRSP is a fairly basic procedure. It goes something like this:

1. Arrive at the financial institution or planner's place of business.
2. Create a proper long-term investing strategy.
3. Fill in the forms needed to set up an RRSP.
4. Take out your chequebook.
5. Write a cheque for your contribution.
6. Tear it out, neatly, and give it to the banker/advisor.
7. Leave.

That's it. Go forth, my child, and toast thine own cleverness and thrift.

Okay, so there could be a few wrinkles. I can just hear Rhoda asking me what she's supposed to do if she doesn't have the money. If you can't simply write a cheque, you still have a few options for adding assets to an RRSP.

Transfer existing non-registered assets. Certain assets such as Canada savings bonds, mutual funds, Treasury bill funds, GICs (sometimes) and Canadian stocks and bonds can all be transferred directly into an RRSP. Assets such as paintings, your 1976 Day-Glo "Makin' Bacon" statuette, gold bullion, certain shares and Air Miles cannot. Take the allowable assets down to your favourite money store and exchange them for RRSP versions of themselves. This is called an "in kind" deposit and you will get an RRSP receipt for the contribution.

Be aware that moving assets from an open account to an RRSP may trigger a taxable capital gain if the asset has appreciated in value. The CCRA considers any assets moved into your RRSP as "sold." If you bought a $3 stock that's worth $4.50 by the time you move it into your RRSP, you will owe tax on the $1.50 gain per share. If the shares have decreased in value, from $4.50 to $3, there is a capital loss. Unfortunately, the CCRA will not allow you to claim a capital loss unless you sell the shares for cash and then deposit that cash into the RRSP. (Get help on this one; it can be tricky.)

Get an RRSP loan. During the RRSP season (usually January and February), loans can be arranged at the bank counter. Most financial institutions quickly approve RRSP loans and offer great rates and very flexible payment plans. Two of my banks have even offered to approve a loan over the phone. Brokers, planners and fund companies are also getting into the loan business, but the interest charged is likely to be higher.

Many banks will allow you to delay repayment for up to 90 days. This allows you to use your refund (refund, not gift!) to repay the loan. In many cases, this will eliminate the need for out-of-pocket payments. Of course, you are still charged interest for those 90 days, so if you can start payments right away, you'll reduce the interest charges and stretch the payments over 12 months rather than nine.

A word of caution: Do not take out an RRSP loan for more than a year. Next year you will need another loan and then another the year after that. Eventually you will fall too far behind. If you can't afford a one-year loan, you need to consider contributing less or adjusting your income or spending habits.

If you are already in debt, then you may as well make the most of it. If you have $1,000 set aside for an RRSP but you're carrying a credit card balance with The Bay, you are better off putting that $1,000 toward the credit card and borrowing for the RRSP. The RRSP loan will charge something like 9%, while the credit card is probably costing you 28%.

Do not take out an RRSP loan for more than a year. Next year you will need another loan and then another the year after that.

Self-Directed RRSPs (SDRRSPs)

The self-directed RRSP is simply an RRSP set up with a particular company, bank or brokerage firm. The "self" portion of the name does not mean that you are on your own (you can still have an advisor to help you out); it means that the individual investment choices are made by you, and that they are not tied to the products pushed by any one company. SDRRSPs usually have an annual fee of between $50 and $300, depending on what investments are required.

Some companies (such as banks and mutual fund firms) also offer an in-house version of the SDRRSP. In these cases, your investment choices are limited to products offered by the institution. In exchange for this limitation, there is generally no administration fee. If you're just starting out, this is probably all the RRSP you need. You can play with the other SDRRSP paperwork later in life!

The SDRRSP offers two big advantages. It allows you to keep all of your RRSP investments in one place and to keep a close eye on your foreign content. This is important because the foreign content allowance of an RRSP is calculated on a per plan basis and there are limits (the CCRA can fine you if you go "over"). After this next section on foreign content, we'll look at a SIMS study that examines the SDRRSP in this context.

The SDRRSP offers two big advantages. It allows you to keep all of your RRSP investments in one place and to keep a close eye on your foreign content.

Foreign Content

According to CCRA rules, you are allowed to invest 30% of your RRSP assets in non-Canadian investments. Since Canadian companies make up a very small percentage of the world's companies, it is advisable to use that 30% to tap into the growth that is happening in America, Asia and Europe.

Historically, the global stock markets have consistently outperformed the TSE. Over the last 20 years, the figures have looked like this:

Stock Market Index	Average Yearly Return (June 1981–June 2001)	$10,000 invested in June 1981 grew to:
TSE 300	9.25%	$58,724
Morgan Stanley Capital International (MSCI) World (CDN $)	14.41%	$147,588
Dow Jones Industrial Average	17.74%	$262,256

S I M S   S T U D Y

Cherry's ex-husband, Larry, really liked a particular U.S. stock mutual fund and wanted to hold as much of it as possible inside his investments. According to the CCRA rules, however, only 30% of his RRSP investments could be outside Canada. Larry had $120,000 in RRSP funds at his local branch and $30,000 with a stockbroker, for a total of $150,000. Reasoning that 30% of $150,000 was $45,000, he asked his broker to use the $30,000 to buy the American fund. The broker refused, explaining that the most he could buy was $9,000, because each RRSP has to track its foreign content separately. Larry's only other option was to move the two RRSPs together into a single SDRRSP. He transferred the bank funds into his brokerage account, for a total of $150,000, giving him a

> total foreign content limit of $45,000. He then used $30,000 to buy the U.S. fund. Then, of course, Cherry took half in the divorce settlement.

Spousal RRSPs

One of the big advantages of marriage (common-law or otherwise) is the spousal RRSP. In a blinding flash of insight, the government called these plans "spousal" RRSPs because you buy them for your spouse! (I warn you now that the word "spouse" ranks up there with "smock" as one of my favourite words to say. Yet I don't like the word "Spock." Strange.)

One of the big advantages of marriage (common-law or otherwise) is the spousal RRSP.

I'm going to use my fictional self and fictional wife as fictional examples. Thus we should be considered an alleged example that in no way reflects what we as an actual couple are actually doing with our RRSPs. Supposedly.

A spousal RRSP is a plan that I (remember, fictional "I") set up in my wife's (ditto) name listing myself as a contributor. That way, the assets build in her (alleged; okay, you get the idea) name while I get the tax deduction. When the money is drawn at retirement, it is counted as her income, not mine!

I set this up for two reasons. The first has to do with the Year of the Rat and I won't go into that. The second has to do with the years of retirement income, which I *will* tell you all about. Assume I retire today to Quebec. With only my RRSP, I would have an annual income of $80,000. Assume also that my wife has no income beyond the generous government benefits. These circumstances would leave me owing roughly $28,000 as tax (see page 157). Bang!

Now let's look at it another way. Let's say that, years ago, I set up a spousal RRSP. Let's say that I contributed the same amount over the years, but divided it equally between my own RRSP and the spousal plan. Now, on retirement, both my wife and I would declare incomes of $40,000, putting us in a lower tax bracket. Together, we owe a grand total of $22,000 in taxes. By simply splitting our retirement income, we saved $6,000! Get it? If you're skimming and hate following numbers, then focus on this:

**By splitting our income, we save $6,000 in taxes
every year of our retirement. We save $6,000!**

This strategy works very well even if both spouses have an income (unlike in the alleged example above). As long as you contribute more on behalf of the spouse who will have less at retirement, the process works. For example, if my wife had a private pension, an annuity or some other form of income that would kick in at retirement, she could arrange a spousal RRSP so that her contributions would grow in my name until my future RRSP income would equal her future pension income. Then we could adjust the contributions every year to keep the monies balanced—some years in her name, some years in mine. Both of us would have an RRSP of our own and a spousal RRSP on each other. Cozy, isn't it?

This whole procedure requires some planning. The trickiest part is to get a spouse. Even trickier, you have to find a spouse you expect to be with at retirement. (Otherwise, this whole plan is really just pre-paid alimony.) Once this is sorted out, you have to estimate how much your current retirement funds will be worth when you actually retire (see Chapter 3). If you have a pension, you can factor in that information as well. (We'll discuss pensions on pages 146–49.)

RRSPs Defiled

Despite everything I've been preaching about the long-term benefits of RRSPs and the need for a long-term outlook, RRSPs can have a few very specific short-term uses. I base the following recommendations on the fact that people should already be saving for these short-term goals separately from their long-term retirement investing. If you use the following plans, programs and schemes to withdraw money from your *real* retirement investing assets, you are a bad, bad person and you can't come to live at my house when you're old.

Buying a house. The Home Buyer's Plan (HBP) is a federally sponsored program that allows you to borrow up to $20,000 from your RRSP to buy a home. If you have a spouse, he or she can also borrow up to $20,000 from their RRSP to buy the same house, meaning that up to $40,000 can be put toward such a purchase. And here's the best part: The money does not have to be for the down payment. You can use it for furniture, landscaping or even that trip you're going to need to recover from the ordeal of unpacking. The CCRA doesn't care—as long as you are actually purchasing a house. The money must be repaid over the following 15 years at the rate of $\frac{1}{15}$th a year.

Normally, I think the HBP is a dicey proposition since you lose long-term growth merely to save on the mortgage. If you cash in an RRSP earning 11% to save on a 6.9%

mortgage, you are actually falling behind in the growth of your total net worth. But, if you've already been saving for a down payment or have a lump sum ready to go, it makes sense to plop it in the RRSP and squeeze

If you cash in an RRSP earning 11% to save on a 6.9% mortgage, you are actually falling behind in the growth of your total net worth.

more money from the increased tax deduction! Let's say that you are currently saving $250 a month in a money market fund for your down payment (using the short-term savings strategy described in Chapter 3). Now let's say that this $250 is preventing you from maximizing your RRSP contribution. You would be far better off to move that money market fund (and its ongoing monthly contributions) into an RRSP. Think of this as a separate "temporary RRSP," and when you get that extra tax refund, you can also use it for the down payment.

If you decide to try this, be careful of a couple of things. First, try to not find your dream house until 90 days after the RRSP deposit. If you take the money out any sooner, you'll lose part of the tax deduction. Second, although the HBP has been around for quite a few years, it could end at any time. If this happens, the money you've put into the plan will be taxed when it is pulled out. To safeguard against this, you could save outside your temporary RRSP until the annual budget is announced (usually in late February). Once you've determined that the plan is still in effect, plop the accumulated cash into the temporary RRSP—keeping that 90-day waiting period in mind. You'll need to be quick if you want to learn about the latest budget and get those assets into the RRSP in time, so be careful with this.

If you've actually used the home buyer's plan and are

now making repayments, don't pay any more than the minimum amount. Since the HBP "loan to yourself" is interest-free, you are usually better off using any extra money to contribute to your long-term-savings RRSP (and thus getting the deduction) or to pay off other debts. You do want to replace the lost capital as quickly as possible, but you also want to direct your money to an area that will provide the most benefits.

Getting an education. Withdrawing from an RRSP has always been an option in determining how to pay for an education. Your reduced income and added education tax credits offset the income created when you cash in the RRSP. The only downside used to be the loss of RRSP room for future contributions. But thanks to the relatively new Lifelong Learning Program (LLP), you can now borrow up to $10,000 a year for education (to a maximum of $20,000) with no loss of RRSP contribution room. As with the home buyer's plan, there is a 15-year repayment plan.

So...the same reasoning and strategy can be applied. If you were saving for school anyway and not maximizing your RRSP contributions, put the savings already accumulated into a temporary RRSP and get the tax break. Just make sure that your education qualifies and that you can use the money as you see fit—for tuition, books, a car or a trip to Las Vegas.

Splitting spousal income. If you put money into a spousal RRSP and wait three years before withdrawing, the money is taxed in your spouse's name, not yours. This can be used at retirement, but it can also come in handy earlier in the game.

Let's say your wife was going to stop working in five years to look after your future kids. She makes $22,000 a year and you make $74,000. This year, you are planning to contribute $5,000 to your RRSP. You have several options. You could put that $5,000 into her RRSP, give her the deduction and have that money available when the child arrives. You could also put the money into a spousal RRSP, get a larger tax deduction (based on your income), and still have it taxed in her name when she withdraws it down the road.

If your wife doesn't work, income splitting is an excellent strategy to consider implementing every few years. Every three years, say, you deposit $10,000 into a spousal RRSP. When the three-year waiting period is up, your wife can pull the money out of the RRSP but keep it invested elsewhere. She pays a bit of tax on the withdrawal, but the money continues to grow outside the RRSP, where it has no future tax liability. This may generate a bit of investment income, but since this is taxed in her name (and since she has no income), who cares?

There is, however, one glitch. At least 24 months and one day must pass between the last spousal RRSP contribution and the date of withdrawal. Otherwise, the income is "attributed" back to the person who claimed the deduction. For example, if I deposit $5,000 to my wife's RRSP on December 31, 1993, she can withdraw the money on January 1, 1996, and have it taxed in her name. If I wait one more day to deposit or she pulls it out one day early, I pay the tax on that income. This applies even if you have three spousal RRSPs set up at three different institutions. It is also pro-rated so that if I put in another $1,000 on November 4, 1994, $1,000 would be attributed back to me—even though the $5,000 my wife is withdrawing has been in the RRSP for the minimum time.

Use an investment account, an RRSP or a Homer-sized pickled egg jar—I could care less. Just grow your savings, build your assets and gather ye rosebuds while ye may.

As a planner, my job is to help people build assets for their financial goals— retirement or whatever else they might be. I like RRSPs and highly recommend them, but what matters most to me is the savings, not the vehicle. Use an investment account, an RRSP or a Homer-sized pickled egg jar—I could care less. Just grow your savings, build your assets and gather ye rosebuds while ye may.

Registered Pension Plans

Let's talk about modern urban myths for a moment. Aside from the one about buying a Chihuahua in Tijuana, only to discover that it's actually a rat, or the one about giant alligators in the sewers, one of the most entertaining begins like this:

> "Oh, uh, no. I don't need any retirement savings. You see, my company has a Pension."

Alright, it's not that funny when it's written down because you're missing the inflection. Usually people will say this with a totally straight face and make me think, just for a moment, that they're being serious. It cracks me up. And they usually say "pension" sort of reverently, with a capital "P."

In case some of you are missing the joke, let me give you some background. We are now talking about the Registered Pension Plans that many companies and government departments offer their staff.

Don't get me wrong: A pension is a nice little perk because it provides a guaranteed, stable income to those who are retired. However, pensions are designed to be of the maximum benefit to those who start at one company when they're 20 and leave when they're 65. Every time you change jobs, you lose some of the long-term benefit. And even if you *were* at one job long enough to build up a half-decent pension income, the retirement income is guaranteed to be only two-thirds of your average working income. Furthermore, few pension plans are tied to inflation, so the income stays flat as your costs escalate over the years. So while the pension plan *can* form a secure, stable base for your retirement income, it had better not be your *only* income.

while the pension plan can form a secure, stable base for your retirement income, it had better not be your only income.

Registered Pension Plans (RPPs) are regulated by different provincial agencies and can have any number of features, restrictions and options. There are two broadly defined types of RPPs: the defined benefit (DB) plan and the defined contribution (DC) plan. For a breakdown of the differences between these two types of plans, check out the box on page 148.

If you are involved in a company pension program, you should gather as much information as you can about your plan. Ask your human resources department the following questions:

A Handy Pension Chart

Defined Benefit Plan	Defined Contribution Plan
Specifies how much income you will receive at retirement (dependent on your working history, earnings, age, etc.)	Specifies how much will be contributed by you and your employer.
Retirement income is guaranteed by the company, which makes up any shortfall.	Retirement income is dependent on the growth of your assets over your career.
Plan usually accumulates units, which are calculated as a percentage of income.	Plan value is listed as a dollar figure.
Company assets are not available to employee until the plan "vests" (which usually takes two years of full-time employment).	Company assets are not available to employee until the plan "vests" (usually takes two years of full-time employment).
Vested assets cannot be withdrawn, only transferred to another pension or a locked-in retirement account.	Vested assets cannot be withdrawn, only transferred to another pension or a locked-in retirement account.
Contributions are considered "pension adjustments" and reduce your RRSP room correspondingly.	Contributions are considered "pension adjustments" and reduce your RRSP room correspondingly.
Benefits are limited by legislation to provide a maximum of $1,722.22 per year of service.	There are no limitations on asset size.

- What kind of pension do I have?
- What are my investment options (for DC plans)?
- Is the plan indexed to inflation, either formally or informally? (If this doesn't seem important, go talk to one of the "urban miners" living in a nearby dumpster: He was given a perfectly adequate $300 a month pension in 1982.)
- What will my retirement income be? Your pension administrator should be able to work out a rough projection. You will need this information to make your retirement projection (see Chapter 3) accurate.

If you left a pension plan any time after 1997, you may be eligible for a Pension Adjustment Reversal (PAR) which will increase your RRSP deduction limit. This is due to the fact that the pension administrators were estimating the current value of your pension based on your working at the company until retirement. If you left early, some of that value is lost and the government has, in effect, overestimated the pension adjustment. Now they owe you. This is surprisingly fair legislation that was nice of the government to implement. If eligible, you will receive a PAR notice at the end of the year in which you quit the pension plan.

Registered Education Savings Plans

Like an RRSP, a Registered Education Savings Plan (RESP) is an umbrella—a place where your investments can grow in a tax-deferred environment. The key difference is that with an RESP, you are saving for your child's education, not yourself. Parents may contribute $4,000 a year into the plan, to a maximum of $42,000 per child. Unlike the RRSP system, there is no foreign content limit. When the RESP is cashed out—hopefully by your university- or college-enrolled child—the money is taxed in his or her hands.

One of the things that always used to irritate my clients about the RESP program (aside from the dull brochures) was the fact that, unlike the other "R" programs, there was no tax deduction on the money contributed. I would explain that, in the case of the RESP, the "R" referred to the registration that allowed for tax-free growth. They would look at me for a moment and respond with a succinct, "Whoopee."

In 1997 and 1998, the federal government revamped the RESP program by enacting a number of changes—the most important of which was the introduction of the Canada Education Savings Grant (CESG). Although it's still not a tax deduction, the CESG does reward contributors with a 20% bonus on the first $2,000 of each year's contributions for each child (to a maximum of $400 each). What this means is that, if you put $2,000 into your daughter's RESP, the federal government will kick in $400. Over 18 years, this amounts to $7,200 of *free money* from Ottawa; and, as Jack Nicholson said in *The Witches of Eastwick*, "That ain't hay!" If you don't have $2,000 to contribute this year, you can plop in the $700 that you can afford and carry $1,300 over to the next year.

If you put $2,000 into your daughter's RESP, the federal government will kick in $400. over 18 years, this amounts to $7,200 of <u>free money</u> from Ottawa.

There were other changes as well: The definition of qualifying educational institutions was broadened and provisions were made for cases where the child chose not to attend post-secondary school. Prior to 1997, any growth that had accumulated within the RESP was lost if your child did not attend school. Under the new rules, up to $50,000 of the RESP's growth can be rolled into an RRSP in the subscriber's name—provided that you have the contribution room. If you don't, the money can simply be withdrawn, though you will pay income tax plus 20% on this amount.

There are a few rules and regulations that go along with this (sort of) free money deal. The CESG is available only if the beneficiary is under the age of 18, and there are certain restrictions if the beneficiary is currently 16 or 17. The beneficiary must also have a SIN number. Unlike RRSPs, contributions must be made within the calendar year (and should be done as early as possible to allow maximum growth).

Getting the Most Out of RESPs

Given the projected increase in costs universities are facing—and with grants and other financial support being reduced—we can expect tuition to rise at a much higher rate than inflation. In Alberta, for example, tuition fees have already risen more than 8% per year in the last five years. To keep ahead of these costs, investors must be prepared to either contribute large amounts of capital (far beyond the $4,000 per year allowance) or gear their investments to higher-growth vehicles such as equities, at least in the early years.

When choosing investment vehicles for your RESP, consider adding equities or bonds, either directly or through mutual funds. This will help to maximize your return on the investments until they are needed for education expenses. Like the RRSP, the RESP protects the investor from having to claim any kind of capital gain or other income. Unfortunately, it also "protects" the investor from realizing any sort of tax deduction for a capital loss. Just as importantly, there is no way to "replace" lost capital if the investment completely disappears. The challenge is thus to find an asset mix that will help offset the erosion of rising costs without placing the assets themselves in jeopardy.

Between this rock of rising costs and the hard place of the limited time frame, the simplest solution is to gradually adjust the asset mix of the RESP over time. It can mutate from a long-term investment program to a short-term savings vehicle as the withdrawal period draws nigh. This is how Cherry chose to plot her son's education funding.

SIMS STUDY

When Cherry decided she wanted to set up an RESP for Chance, she visited her financial planner and created a specific needs analysis. (You can do this yourself with software like Quicken, a spreadsheet or even a website featuring a Java-based calculator.)

Once she had a "best guess" about how much money Chance would need, she set up both an RESP and a simple "in trust for" (ITF) account. Cherry's parents deposited $2,000 worth of a steady, blue chip global equity fund into the RESP. Meanwhile, Cherry set up a small monthly purchase plan for the ITF account, buying into a higher-risk emerging markets fund and a technology fund. This mix, regularly reviewed, will stay essentially the same over the next dozen or so years.

When Chance becomes a teenager, Cherry will start purchasing aggressive funds and looking for opportunities to roll those assets into more conventional blue chip funds. ("Opportunities" would be defined as years with above-average returns, say 10% or more.)

Once Chance is 15 or 16, Cherry needs to start thinking of the RESP as a short-term savings plan. She will now move most of its assets into global bonds or possibly a U.S. T-bill. The ITF assets will all be moved to blue chip equity investments to keep Cherry's taxes low.

Around Chance's 18th birthday, Cherry will transfer the ITF assets to him at the rate of three to one— meaning that for every dollar Chance earns and saves for school on his own, Cherry will "gift" him $3 from the ITF. (One of my clients did this with his son, and I think it's an excellent carrot to dangle in front of a teenager. It quadruples the income he is earning from his part-time job and makes saving for school easier. But the fact that the education money is not just a gift reinforces the value of education.)

But regardless of the drawbacks and limitations, the RESP program should be considered as the core strategy for any saving you are doing for your kids.

Once Chance starts school, Cherry will redeem the RESP first to ensure that its assets are gone by the time he graduates. He can then use the ITF assets for anything— starting his own RRSP, buying a flashy car to impress chicks or acquiring a chicken-plucking franchise (assuming there are chickens in 2023).

This is not the only way to manage an RESP. There are as many strategies as there are investors. But regardless of the drawbacks and limitations, the RESP program should be considered as the core strategy for any saving you are doing for your kids.

Education Saving Tips and Tricks

- Once you set up an ITF account for your children, you cannot withdraw the money for personal use. It invalidates any past tax savings.
- It makes sense to build your RESP assets to a maximum of $2,000 before starting an ITF. This allows you to automatically receive the CESG maximum.
- If you have been saving only in an ITF, you could move $2,000 from that account into a newly formed RESP to receive the CESG bonus, but there may be tax consequences, as this will most likely create a capital gain. There are also special rules if the transfer creates a capital loss. Although you are allowed to deposit up to $4,000 in an RESP, this may not always be advisable. Since the CESG will be paid only on deposits up to $2,000—and since transferring money from an ITF to an RESP can create tax problems—you may want to leave current funds in the ITF and make only new contributions to the RESP.

7 Income Tax
one-on-one with the CCRA

> "Taxes are the fine we pay for thriving."
> —*Anon*

AS PEOPLE ENTER THE WORKFORCE, they are suddenly confronted with a heretofore ignored fact of daily life called income tax. It is important that you grow to love paying income tax early on, because you are going to have to do it for the rest of your life (*and* for the year after that). If you can't manage to embrace the practice, you will either develop a nervous tic or be forced to live on a tropical tax haven—I mean island—in the Caribbean.

Canada has a complex, overbearing, clunky, one-sided and onerous system of taxation that is nonetheless loved by financial planners, tax lawyers and accountants because they (uh, okay, we) make money helping people pay less in taxes. If the government simply dropped the rates and reduced the average tax return to a manageable 50 pages, a lot of us advisor types would go broke. Luckily, the system is so entrenched in our collective psyche that it will outlast us all.

In a recent study, the Fraser Institute determined that

between 1961 and 2000, the average Canadian family's total tax bill rose from 33.5% to 47.5% of its income—and this is down slightly from the peak year of 1997, when tax bills totalled 48.7% of all income. (It should be noted that this study included all of the taxes a family might pay, not just the income variety.)

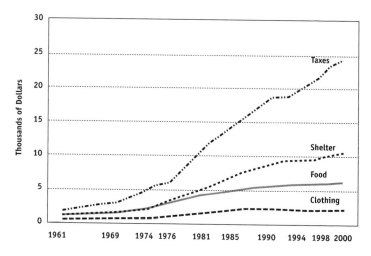

In light of this somewhat staggering figure, it should come as no surprise to learn that Canadians spend more on taxes than they do on clothing, food and shelter (see graph). Despite the ridiculous amount of money that most of us put into taxes, the system is still labelled "progressive." In no way, shape or form does this refer to actual progress; it simply means that as your income increases, the percentage of tax you pay also grows. According to the Fraser Institute, Canadian families with incomes above $63,000 (representing one-third of the country's population) paid nearly two-thirds of all the country's taxes. The bottom third, on the other hand, paid only 4.3%.

How Much Tax? Individual Tax Table for 2001*

The upper portion of this table shows the combined federal and provincial (or territorial) income taxes payable, including surtaxes. The calulations assume that only the basic personal tax credit is available and that all income is either interest or ordinary income (such as salary).

2001	Federal Income Tax	B.C.	Alberta	Sask.	Manitoba	Ontario	Quebec	N.B.	N.S.	P.E.I.	Nfld.	Yukon	N.T. & Nunavut	Non-resident
$1,000,000	$281,509	$442,748	$380,219	$438,489	$452,355	$449,250	$476,067	$455,245	$460,296	$460,574	$473,437	$417,177	$408,187	$416,6330
$500,000	$136,509	$214,248	$185,219	$213,489	$220,355	$217,202	$232,492	$221,045	$223,611	$223,724	$230,228	$202,142	$197,937	$202,033
$400,000	$107,509	$168,548	$146,219	$168,489	$173,955	$170,792	$183,777	$174,205	$176,274	$176,354	$181,586	$159,135	$155,887	$159,113
$300,000	$78,509	$122,848	$107,219	$123,489	$127,555	$124,383	$135,062	$127,365	$128,937	$128,984	$132,945	$116,128	$113,837	$116,193
$250,000	$64,009	$99,998	$87,719	$100,989	$104,355	$101,178	$110,704	$103,945	$105,268	$105,299	$108,624	$94,625	$92,812	$94,733
$200,000	$49,509	$77,148	$68,219	$78,489	$81,155	$77,973	$86,347	$80,525	$81,600	$81,614	$84,303	$73,121	$71,787	$73,273
$150,000	$35,009	$54,298	$48,719	$55,989	$57,955	$54,768	$61,989	$57,105	$57,931	$57,929	$59,982	$51,618	$50,762	$51,813
$100,000	$20,509	$31,448	$29,219	$33,489	$34,755	$31,564	$37,632	$33,685	$34,263	$34,244	$35,661	$30,114	$29,737	$30,353
$90,000	$17,909	$27,178	$25,619	$29,289	$30,415	$27,223	$33,011	$29,433	$29,829	$29,807	$31,097	$26,258	$25,967	$26,505
$80,000	$15,309	$22,958	$22,019	$25,089	$26,075	$22,882	$28,390	$25,181	$25,395	$25,370	$26,533	$22,403	$22,197	$22,657
$70,000	$12,709	$18,788	$18,419	$20,889	$21,735	$18,541	$23,769	$20,929	$21,120	$20,933	$21,968	$18,554	$18,427	$18,809
$60,000	$10,169	$14,909	$14,879	$16,749	$17,468	$14,433	$19,198	$16,763	$16,914	$16,605	$17,465	$14,847	$14,745	$15,050
$50,000	$7,969	$11,659	$11,679	$13,199	$13,648	$11,192	$14,976	$13,081	$13,205	$12,912	$13,612	$11,635	$11,555	$11,794
$40,000	$5,769	$8,409	$8,479	$9,649	$9,828	$8,068	$11,014	$9,399	$9,510	$9,332	$9,796	$8,423	$8,365	$8,538
$30,000	$3,614	$5,220	$5,324	$6,144	$6,082	$5,014	$7,090	$5,801	$5,860	$5,828	$6,025	$5,277	$5,240	$5,349
$20,000	$2,014	$2,890	$2,649	$3,394	$3,367	$2,794	$3,884	$3,233	$3,212	$3,248	$3,345	$2,941	$2,920	$2,981
Top (2001) marginal rates	29.00%	45.70%	39.00%	45.00%	46.40%	46.41%	48.72%	46.84%	47.34%	47.37%	48.64%	43.01%	42.05%	42.92%
Dividend Tax Credit	13.33%	19.23%	19.73%	21.33%	19.33%	21.34%	21.96%	20.93%	21.80%	21.80%	23.14%	19.77%	19.33%	19.73%
Max value of add'l credits	16.00%	23.30%	26.00%	27.50%	26.90%	25.67%	34.86%	25.68%	26.75%	26.78%	27.52%	23.73%	23.20%	23.68%

Taxable Income (row label)

* This table is reproduced, with permission, from *Tax Facts and Figures for Individuals and Corporations (2001)*, published by PricewaterhouseCoopers, who retain the copyright.

The table on page 157 illustrates the point. It shows the federal tax rates you pay on various income levels.

Timeless Tax Tips for Today and (Maybe) Tomorrow

As the CCRA has grown smarter and hungrier over the years, the noose has tightened around the neck of the average employed Canadian. These days, there are very few loopholes left to facilitate any sort of tax strategy. However, there are still a few basic tactics that can be used to help lessen the tax thump.

One word of caution: It's very important not to be lulled into a sense of complacency if your tax return shows you don't owe any money. Remember that you have been paying taxes for the entire year, effectively giving the government some of your money to blow for more than 12 months. You should work hard to ensure they get absolutely no more than they're legally owed.

The following tips are effective according to today's tax rules. If it's 2005 and you are snooping through an old, dog-eared 2001 edition—hopefully worth a fortune—before filing your 2004 tax return, good luck. I hope the CCRA fines will teach you that buying a fresh new copy would have been easier.

File a return every year. If you've earned an income that's near the personal exemption mark and you haven't filed a return, you'll get a snippy little reminder from the CCRA. If you don't, it's probably because they owe you money. I come across this situation every year with students who haven't bothered to file. At the very least, grab a return, sign it and send it in blank. You'll lose some deductions, but if you get back at least as much as you spent on postage, you're ahead of the game—and you'll be notified of your RRSP contribution limit for the next year. Another good reason to file a return? You are required to do so by law.

Get an RRSP. It makes me silently giggle when people will squawk squawk squawk all day long about Canada's high tax rates and then not take full advantage of the registered retirement savings plan. Few countries have a program as large, as flexible and as generous—use it!

Get outta town. Moving expenses are deductible if you move at least 40 kilometres closer to your work and you weren't reimbursed by your company. For example, moving from an acreage half an hour north of the city to a house downtown would qualify if you worked in the city. Moving expenses include hotel and food bills, the movers, selling costs, legal fees and lease cancellation fees, among other things.

You can also claim moving expenses if you are a student who is moving to start a job or full-time post-secondary education.

You can also claim moving expenses if you are a student who is moving to start a job or full-time post-secondary education. However, in the latter case, you can claim the deduction only if you have income from a scholarship or grant.

Get an education. Students who do not use the education and tuition credits can transfer up to $850 worth of credits to a spouse (or parent or grandparent). Furthermore, all interest charged on student loans is tax-deductible. If you made monthly payments of $125, and $25 from each payment was deemed to be interest, then a year's worth of payments would generate a $300 tax deduction (12 x $25 = $300).

Income Splitting

I was going to lump this in with the Timeless Tax Tips, but it's such a good one it deserves its own section. Specifically, I want to focus on the various methods of income splitting that are available and legal (the best income splitting ideas are the ones the CCRA has the most problems with... sigh). And remember: You don't need a marriage contract to have a spouse. If you have lived conjugally (wink, wink) with someone for at least a year and they have credits they can't use (tuition, medical expenses), you should try to use them. Think as a team! Get something out of the relationship!

Why Split Incomes?

You already know the answer to this question. As we saw in the section on spousal RRSPs, the more you make (or report), the higher the percentage of taxes you have to pay. It doesn't take a brain surgeon to figure out that you'll pay less in taxes on two incomes of $50,000 than on one income of $100,000. This doesn't work as well for really high-income earners: Splitting a $300,000 income into two $150,000 incomes doesn't reduce the tax bill because both incomes are still in the highest tax bracket. (But if you *are* currently making $300,000, I don't want to hear any whining!) It does, however, offer other benefits, such as doubling RRSP contributions, personal exemptions, etc.

Income splitting strategies work best where one spouse has a relatively high income and the other has little or none. If you are a single person with dependants, a few opportunities are still available. If you are a single, employed person with no spouse or dependants, then maximize your RRSP, go find someone and settle down. (I mean, really, would it kill you to call her?)

Income Splitting Tips

All of the tips presented here are general ideas and should be implemented only after consulting a professional about your specific situation. As we go through this information, I am going to use three acronyms: HIP (higher income partner), LIP (lower income partner) and ISO (income splitting opportunity). This will save me some typing, which is good, because I'm very slow.

- **The spousal RRSP.** This is the simplest and cleanest ISO. The HIP starts an RRSP in the LIP's name to split retirement income (and the taxes paid on it). See Chapter 6 for more details.
- **Divide and conquer.** Assuming that the LIP has at least some income, have the LIP do all of the non-RRSP investing while the HIP pays all bills (including the LIP's income tax, if possible). All future gains from these non-registered investments are taxable in the LIP's name and thus should attract less tax. For example:

S I M S   S T U D Y

If Fred earns $50,000 a year and Wilma earns $8,000, they can reasonably invest $8,000 a year and claim it in Wilma's name. If this $8,000 earns $800, it would be considered her income and taxed in her name. But thanks to her low overall income, she may not end up paying tax on the money. If the $800 was in Fred's name, he might owe $300 or $400.

- **Hire a spouse.** If the HIP is self-employed, she could pay the LIP an income to assist with her business.
- **Get the most out of your child.** Money set aside for a child should be structured to generate capital gains rather than interest or dividends. Capital gains cannot be attributed back to you. This means that bonds and preferred shares may create future tax problems while company shares or equity mutual funds will not. Of course, tax treatment should be only one factor you consider when you're choosing investment options.
- **Use the equivalent-to-spouse deduction.** If you are single, divorced, separated or widowed, support a dependant and live with the dependant in a home you maintain, you can claim up to $6,100 as a deduction. Cherry, who supports her son Chance, uses this deduction to offset the extra income she must claim because of support payments from her ex-husband.
- **Share medical expenses.** Medical expenses include tests, prescribed drugs, private medical plan premiums (such as Blue Cross), some travelling expenses, attendants, nursing home fees, glasses, dentures, etc. To

qualify for a deduction, these expenses must be paid for out of your pocket, not by the provincial health plans. Medical expenses should be claimed on the LIP's return. This is because the expenses must total 3% of your income before you can claim a credit. Thus, if one spouse earns $10,000 a year and claims $350 of medical costs while the other earns $50,000 and claims $500, the only deduction is $50 for the LIP ($350 less 3% of $10,000, or $300). The HIP would have no deduction for any expenses under $1,500 (3% of $50,000). By combining the two amounts on the LIP's return, the couple ensures that the LIP will receive $550 in tax credits ($850 less 3% of $10,000, or $300).

It's also worth remembering that you can pick any 12-month period ending in the tax year to claim medical expenses. This can help maximize the amount of your claim. For example, if you have $4,000 of dental work done in December 2000 and $1,500 more in January 2001, you may wish to combine these two in your 2001 tax year. This way, you don't have to pass the 3% rule twice.

- **Be charitable.** You can lump charitable donations together over a five-year period and claim them on the HIP's return. Donations under $200 receive a smaller tax credit than donations over that amount. Combining donations on one return means that you need to get past the lower deduction limit only once.

Though going to see an accountant deters many people, a fee of $250 seems like small potatoes if it saves you $3,000.

- **Child care.** Only the LIP can claim child care expenses
  including baby-sitting, nursery school, and certain day
  camps and boarding schools. Deductions for child care
  expenses change frequently, but as of 2001, the limit
  was $7,000 per child under the age of seven. If the child
  is disabled, both the amount and the age limit change.

There are many more elaborate options for splitting
income between family members. And while most are suitable only for very specific situations (and require more cash,
time and hassle than can usually be saved on taxes), almost
everyone can make one or two small changes that could
result in future tax savings. For this, and other more complex
matters, you should consider getting professional tax help.
Though going to see an accountant deters many people, a fee
of $250 seems like small potatoes if it saves you $3,000.

8 Retirement and After
one last kick at the can

> "In spite of the cost of living, it's still popular."
> —*Kathy Norris*

AHHH, RETIREMENT—the time when you can sit back and reap the rewards of years of hard work. Let's talk a bit about the resources you'll have when you finally stop working at age 110 or so. I am going to dwell on a few key things that you need to do right now—like drawing up a will and getting enough life insurance—but I'm not going into detail on much else. Let's face it: You have many, many, many, many years of thankless, 60-hour work weeks ahead of you, so why bother?

There are two areas I want to explore: the short time after you stop working when you'll still be alive, and the rest of eternity when you're not.

Alive and Kicking

Assuming you've managed to stop working before you die, you're going to need something to live on. If you don't save a single, solitary cent for your own retirement, you'll be left with a fairly sorry set of options. (Luckily, you've read this book and now know how essential it is to plan ahead.)

Government Benefits

(This will be a short section.)

- **Canada Pension Plan (CPP).** In case you didn't read the introduction, here's a refresher course: the money you are now contributing to CPP is for *current* retirees, not you. By the time you retire, the plan will probably be broke.
- **Old Age Security (OAS).** Forget this plan; it will be toast long before you retire.
- **Guaranteed Income Supplement (GIS).** Ditto.

Registered Plans

When you retire, your RRSP turns into an RRIF (Registered Retirement Income Fund) or an insurance annuity. Both are designed to provide constant, regular retirement income. The key difference is that the annuity provides a guaranteed amount, while the RRIF's payout depends on the growth of the assets inside the plan. During your early retirement years—when substantial growth is still needed—the RRIF's assets should probably be very similar to those in your pre-retirement RRSP. Only later should they be reshuffled into a very conservative mix. When you are drooling and incontinent, you can even consider moving the RRIF to an annuity for the security of the income.

The two biggest problems with annuities today? First, the return is affected by interest rates, and once they are set, they are set. For example, if you buy an annuity when interest rates are low, your payment will be low . . . forever. Second, when you buy an annuity, you can't change your mind and get your money back. Once you have set up the monthly income and decided on your options, that is what you get . . . forever.

Pensions

As we discussed in Chapter 6, a defined benefit plan calculates your payout based on things like how long you worked, your income, etc. A defined contribution plan is generally turned into an annuity. Both usually require you to set up a joint life option so your spouse has some money when you kick off.

Listen Up!
I would strongly suggest that you consider this section merely as a collection of ideas to discuss with your lawyer and financial planner. Most of these matters are regulated provincially, and while the legislation is similar, there are certain strategies that may work well in one province, but are unnecessary or even counterproductive in another.

Death: A Serious Financial Hazard

At the moment of death, individuals are thought of as having disposed of all of their assets (which is true in a very deep and philosophical way). Without some thought and preparation, this deemed disposition can add up to some very heavy tax bills. Not only that, but the money you have spent a lifetime gathering could be shuffled together and plopped into the hands of your lazy, no-good brother-in-law to be blown on turkey smokers, breast-shaped beer glasses and the racetrack! In this section, we are going to discuss two estate matters that you need to settle right away—your will and (if you need it) proper insurance.

Your Will

According to most dictionaries, wills are defined as documents in which a person sets out his or her wishes for the disposal of their estate after death. It's a solemn definition for a solemn topic. Most of us don't even like to think about a will, let alone sit down and actually prepare it. Maybe it reminds us of our inevitable mortality (something no self-respecting 30-year-old wants to consider); or maybe we don't think we need one; or maybe we're just lazy. Whatever excuse you're using to avoid dealing with the topic, it's time to toss it aside. Everyone needs a will.

If you die without one—otherwise known as dying "intestate"—the province appoints an administrator who will pay off your debts and then dole out whatever money is left, usually in the following order:

1. Spouse;
2. Child or children;
3. Grandchildren;
4. Great-grandchildren;
5. Father;
6. Mother; or
7. Brothers and sisters.

If none of these are still around, the province rubs its massive, hungry hands together and uses the obvious-sounding "escheat" process to name itself your beneficiary.

(Haven't they gotten enough of your money over the years?) A will will help you avoid this situation. And don't even start whining about all the time, money and energy this is going to take. Look, a will is easy! Go to a strip mall, find a lawyer, and get him to set up your will. Twenty minutes and $100 later, you'll be done. Before you visit the strip mall lawyer, though, you might want to consider the following points.

> A will is easy! Go to a strip mall, find a lawyer, and get him to set up your will. Twenty minutes and $100 later, you'll be done.

- Make sure your will contains a provision to roll assets over to your spouse. Moving assets to a surviving spouse is a very effective way to defer paying taxes on your assets—including property, a pension, an RRSP or an RRIF. Of course, most lawyers will put this in without being asked. If yours doesn't, find a new lawyer. (All of this assumes that you *want* to give your spouse some dough.)
- If you are living in a common-law or same-sex relationship, your spouse has no recourse under provincial intestacy legislation. If they are not mentioned in the will—or there is no will—they will get whatever your "real" family decides to give them.
- Carefully consider your choice of "personal representative" or executor (or executrix, which sounds way more sexy and, well, domineering, doesn't it?). The ideal person should have the respect of the beneficiaries, no conflict of interest, a good knowledge of your assets and your goals, and a certain competence in their own financial affairs. You should also name a replacement

representative in case the first one is in the dolphin pool with you when Flipper inexplicably turns "rogue."

- If you have children under the age of majority, you should also name a guardian. This may or may not be the same person as the executrix.

- Give your executor enough flexibility to make effective moves—for example, he or she can make a spousal RRSP contribution for you during the first 60 days of the year after you die. Try also to make sure that the executor can invest the proceeds of the estate in a mutual fund. In many provinces, if the will is not worded correctly, the executor cannot "divest investment responsibility" to a professional money manager. This would restrict the executor to making his own stock purchase decisions or confining himself to bonds and GICs.

Power of attorney is granted to a trusted friend or advisor who will manage your financial affairs if you are incapacitated because of an accident, illness or simple, overpowering laziness.

- Non-traditional wills can sometimes be valid. When I first heard the term "holographic will," I immediately thought of the scene in *Star Wars* where that cute little holographic image of Princess Leia pops up from the droid and gives a message to Obi-Wan. In real life, it refers to a handwritten will and it can be deemed valid, provided that it is completely handwritten.

- While you're setting up your will, you should also establish your power of attorney. Power of attorney is granted to a trusted friend or advisor who will manage your financial affairs if you are incapacitated because of an accident, illness or simple, overpowering laziness. (If you are in a coma, it is very difficult to renew the mortgage, even if the bank employee does seem to share your condition.) Make sure the power of attorney is "enduring" or "continuing"; otherwise, it will become invalid the moment you are deemed incompetent. If you have not named someone, the provincial government will. Anyone (your brother, daughter or even Dr. Lazard Malignant, your arch-nemesis) can apply to be appointed.

- To get all the depressing stuff out of the way at the same time, have the strip mall lawyer prepare your living will, as well. A living will is used to communicate your personal health care decisions if you are not in a position to do so. For example, my living will reads something like this:

"Do everything you can to keep me alive. I don't care who else must suffer or what organs must be stolen from Brazil! I want to live. Live, I tell you!"

Seriously, this is where you tell your family and doctors what sort of medical efforts should be made on your behalf. Advising you on this is way beyond the scope of this book, so I'll content myself with telling you to do your family a favour and get one done.

Life Insurance

We've spent a lot of time talking about the various elements of a successful financial plan. One of the key elements must be life insurance. Let me clearly state that I hate life insurance as much as the next person. In fact, I probably hate it more because it's such a hassle to deal with. (Nothing would piss me off more than spending five hours doing a financial plan for a client that depends on her working at a job for the next 33 years, only to find out she was accidentally decapitated playing with the office photocopier. Aside from 47 crisp copies of a really intense, sort of surprised expression on my late client's face, what are we left with? The plan we created needed another 33 years to build up assets, and the time horizon has now been...cut short. The client wanted me to help her get...ahead...and, well, here we are!)

But life insurance is important because it allows you to replace time with money. The basic idea behind insurance is to spend a small portion of something's cost of something to protect you from losing the whole thing. My favourite analogy is car insurance. If a car costs you $25,000, you are well advised to spend $750 (3% of the cost) to replace it if it gets "lost" (stolen, totalled or misplaced in the underground parking lot). Life insurance used to be that simple. In the Middle Ages, you could buy it to last for only a few years (of course, back then you married at 13, were a grandfather by 28 and could look forward to what insurance marketers called "Freedom 35"—which was when most people died). Let's start from scratch.

- **Life insurance replaces the money you are no longer there to earn.** If you worked for 30 years at $50,000 a year, you would have contributed $1.5 million to your household income. Dying in year six deprives your family of $1.2 million they had bargained on. Insurance is designed to replace that income.

    Let's reflect on this for a moment. It may *seem*

obvious, but here is a point that many people have not considered: *If you are a single adult with little or no debt, you probably don't need insurance.* If you have no dependants and no debt, then no one will be "hurt financially" when you kick off.

- **What you buy should be based on your needs, not on how much you can afford.** Too many people own life insurance based on what they can afford each month, not on what they need. If you can't afford to buy the amount of the insurance that your agent really likes, ask if you can get more of the cheaper stuff now and "upgrade" later.

Before buying any insurance, be annoyingly particular about learning the details.

There are several basic types of life insurance. What follows is a brief look at their advantages and disadvantages. I want to emphasize again that the generic policies are discussed here in very general terms. The specifics of your own policy may be quite different, even if the policy has a similar name. Before buying any insurance, be annoyingly particular about learning the details.

Term Insurance

Term insurance is exactly that: insurance you buy for a specific term. These days, most terms are five-, 10- or 20-year periods. Moreover, most term insurance is guaranteed renewable and convertible. This means that once you qualify for your first term, you will automatically requalify for additional terms until the policy ends. The renewed terms (i.e., the second five years) usually have their premiums guaranteed when you purchase the policy. Be aware, however, that not all term insurance has these guarantees. Some run only for a single term; others allow additional terms, but do not guarantee the premium. However, the single-term policies can be a very cheap way to buy insurance for a specific time frame or goal.

Term insurance is best thought of as the closest equivalent to car insurance. If the policyholder dies, the payout works well. But it's a total waste of money if he lives. In other words, if you kick off in the first couple of weeks, term insurance is an amazing investment. The longer you live—and the more premiums you pay—the less of a "deal" it is.

Whole Life Insurance

Whole life insurance charges a level premium for as long as you own the policy. The life insurance company is able to do this by calculating roughly when you're going to die. This is based on a massive database of general statistics and a thorough examination of your particular situation and health. The actuaries at the life insurance company will also do a projection of their administrative costs and what they expect to earn on the dough you give them for premiums.

T-100 Insurance

T-100 insurance—also called "term to 100"—is a modified form of whole life insurance. It is essentially whole life insurance with no cash value. This insurance does not officially cover you for "life," it runs only until you turn 100. Some of these policies pay out the death benefit at age 100, but these have become a lot less popular (with the insurance companies) since more and more people are living past 100!

Universal Life

As with any financial product—or possibly anything in life—universal life policies are neither as good nor as bad as the zealots on either side claim. (I love the word "zealots" and plan to use it in all of my books or until my editor says no.) Universal life goes far beyond mere income replacement and attempts to combine life insurance with a savings or investment element to provide a flexible all-in-one package. It is easiest to think of universal life insurance as a pure insurance policy with a self-directed investment account tacked on.

Universal life has been touted (mostly by life agents and life companies) as the penultimate perfect be-all and end-all, all-in-one, all-around single financial product. It does have many attractive features, but before you commit yourself to the bottom line, you need to consider the downside: Universal life may be more policy than most of us want or need. To maintain the claim of maximum flexibility, universal life must become very complex. When companies introduce a new universal life policy, it is not uncommon for them to offer a full-day seminar to advisors to illustrate the features and possible drawbacks. (And I can tell you from personal experience these seminars are not exactly what you'd call a laugh riot.)

Universal life may be more policy than most of us want or need.

For young clients, I generally suggest a term 10 (T-10) policy. A T-10 policy is usually renewable to age 70 or so, and costs rise (dramatically!) every 10 years. At the beginning of our chosen careers, though, our cash *needs* are high and our cash *reserves* are usually low. Insurance needs also tend to vary dramatically during the first few years of family life (new kids and jobs, new places to live). Given these circumstances, it makes sense to "maximize" insurance purchases through the use of low-cost terms. I should mention again that this is *my own personal plan of action* for those first needing to consider insurance. It probably is not right for everyone, but I believe it's worth considering.

S I M S   S T U D Y

After they express an interest in an insurance policy, Barney the Banker has Fred and Wilma sit down with the estate specialist, Mr. Slate, and prepare an insurance needs analysis.

First: Mr. Slate adds up all Fred and Wilma's debt—including final income taxes, funeral costs and other expenses (setting aside money for the kids' college education, and some more for Wilma's sister, who was born without ears and needs major corrective surgery).

Second: Mr. Slate adds up the money needed to provide the household with the same amount Fred contributes as a wage earner. (This is not exactly the same as Fred's wages, because it's assumed that he spends some of his money on himself.) Mr. Slate also determines what Fred would need to replace the work Wilma does around the house.

Third: Fred, Wilma and Mr. Slate decide that the insurance should pay out for 15 years. They also factor in investments from the insurance process earning 8% a year. Mr. Slate whips all of this information into his computer and comes up with this:

For Fred. (Well, actually for Wilma if Fred were to head to the great gravel pit in the sky.)

Debts		
Final taxes	$3,300	
New ears for sister	$10,000	
Funeral expenses	$8,000	
Total Debts	**$29,300**	
Cash on hand	$2,300	
Group life at work	$64,000	(two times his current salary)
Total Assets	**$66,300**	
Total Assets	$66,300	
Total Debts	($29,300)	
Surplus:	$37,000	

Note: The "Debts" line shows $8,000.

Mr. Slate smiles a steely smile when Fred assumes that he and Wilma are fine. He reminds them that he still needs to subtract the following numbers from that surplus:

Kids' education	$20,000 ($10,000 each, to be invested in a college fund)
Family income needed	$320,000 ($24,000 a year until the unborn children are

20—$24,000 is roughly 70% of Fred's current income and reflects the money he spends on himself each year. The $320,000 figure is a projection based on the "pot" earning an 8% return and lasting for 21 years, rising each year by 4% to keep up with inflation.)

All of this means that Fred needs $303,000 ($340,000 less the $37,000 surplus from his current assets) in addition to the insurance he already has. Looking at a sample T-10 policy, this would currently cost him:

T-10

First 10 years	$289.00 a year
Second 10 years	$626.00 a year
Third 10 years	$1,348/yr
Fourth	$3,780/yr
Fifth (till age 80)	$11,742/yr

The other policies price out as follows:

T-100	$888/yr
Cash value (whole life)	$1,272/yr for 20 years
Universal life	$1,067/yr

Fourth: The insurance program should be reviewed every three to five years or with every new event (the birth of another child, an inheritance, a job loss, a new house). If Fred does buy the T-10 insurance, it also makes sense to review it just before it goes into its second term (when costs jump). Starting a brand-new policy with a brand-new company is usually cheaper than that second term. This strategy will require more forms and probably more blood. If you do choose to buy new insurance, it is very important not to cancel your old policy until you have the new one in your hand. That way, you'll be covered in case you've developed some embarrassing medical problem that makes you ineligible for a new policy.

There are as many insurance strategies as there are policies and there is no single right answer. Before making a decision, make sure you have considered all of your options and gathered as much information as possible from someone you trust (or three people you only partially trust).

Disability Insurance

You are much more likely to be disabled than to die. Modern medicine can allow you to linger far longer than was possible in the past. On March 16, 1999, Rob Carrick wrote the following in *The Globe and Mail*:

You are much more likely to be disabled than to die. Modern medicine can allow you to linger far longer than was possible in the past.

Care for some frightening statistics to underscore the need for disability coverage? The insurance industry is overflowing with them:

• 418 of 1,000 men will be disabled for a period of at least 90 days between the ages of 35 and 65; for women, it's 490...
• At age 40, the chances of being disabled for longer than 90 days are four times greater than dying...
• At age 50, the odds of a man being disabled for more than 90 days is three in 10; for women, it's one in five...
• The average duration of the disability at this age is 3.1 years...
• Almost 50% of all mortgage foreclosures are a result of disability, not death.

I hate life insurance and I believe that people without dependants don't need it. Disability insurance, though, is a different matter altogether. If you are disabled and not able to learn a living, no financial plan in the world is going to help you.

You need disability insurance. Period.

Luckily, disability insurance is available through your work at cheap cheap rates. It is called short-term disability (STD) and long-term disability (LTD). If you are offered these benefits, take them; take as much as you can and don't quibble over price. If you are not offered STD or LTD at work, find it privately. It will be expensive. It will be a hassle. But it's completely worth it. Don't whine. Just pay.

When looking at a disability policy, consider these options:

Run to age 65. You can get disability insurance that will run two years, five years or until you turn 65. I think the two- and five-year options, though far cheaper, are close to useless. If we're talking about a serious medical problem or accident, will two years really do the trick? I try to talk everyone into the "age 65" option.

Elimination period. This refers to the amount of time you have to be off work before beginning to collect. The longer the period of elimination, the lower the premium. The options are 1, 30, 60, 90 or 120 days. The 90-day option is quite a bit cheaper than the three shorter ones and only slightly more expensive than the 120-day option.

COLA rider. This allows you all the Coke or Pepsi you wish while you're in the hospital instead of the generic cola they normally serve. Okay, it's actually the cost-of-living adjustment, and it simply means that if you do start to collect benefits, those benefits will increase over the years to keep up with inflation.

> If you are not offered STD or LTD at work, find it privately. It will be expensive. It will be a hassle. But it's completely worth it. Don't whine. Just pay.

Future income option. This allows you to pay for more insurance coverage in the future without having to requalify. It can be pretty handy if you expect your income to rise quickly over the next few years.

This is only a sampling of the many features you can get on a disability policy, and each company will have different names for these options. Sit down with your advisor and work through the options. You can insure up to 75% of your current income. This is usually more than enough because the proceeds from a private disability policy are tax-free. (Proceeds from your work plan are not.) If you've done a decent budget (no, seriously), then you may want to base your coverage on your monthly needs instead of your salary.

Conclusion
In the End

> "Wealth is the product of man's capacity to think."
> —*Ayn Rand*

IF YOU'VE MADE IT ALL THE WAY TO HERE, you can now e-mail me and let me know. I'll send you an Official Screaming Capitalist Completion Certificate (suitable for framing) that will help you prove to nerdy friends and family that you are no longer a Financial Dweeb. The e-mail address is formerdweeb@screamingcapitalist.com.

In a perfect world, we'd all floss three times a day, do 100 sit-ups every evening, help orphans, be kind, selfless and gentle, *and* follow all of the steps listed in this book. In the *real* world, if you pick up a few new financial habits, strategies or ideas, then this book has done its job and you will have more money later than you would have otherwise. So convinced I am of this that I am going to ask you to send me (now, not later) $20 in sheer, white-pure gratitude.

What I hope I have conveyed and want to reiterate right now is that *all* of this intimidating, fiddly financial stuff is, in the end, pretty simple. With a few facts, some thought and, naturally, a kind, selfless and gentle advisor (poke, poke), it is easy to get going on achieving your financial goals.

Thank you for reading this and good luck!

—*Kevin Cork*

P.S. If you do absolutely nothing else, then at least go out today and start an RRSP for $25 a month, anywhere... please.

Resources and References

ONE OF THE FEW ADVANTAGES that Gen-Xers have over the boomers is the Internet. Despite all the hype and angst over the Web, few people over 40 truly wrap themselves in its resourceful embrace. The Internet—combined with e-mail newsletters and some boxed software—can be a powerful ally in the struggle for financial freedom. Power to the browsers!

Just as this is not your typical money book, this is not going to be your typical resource section. I compiled this chapter after making two basic assumptions. First, if you've managed to hang in through the entire book, there might actually be things you'd like to know more about. Some of the websites and books listed here will help point you to more detailed information on everything from taxes and real estate to lawyers and investment groups. My second assumption is less "professional," if you will. If you're any-thing like me, you occasionally (okay, always) like to be entertained. As such, you'll find some really cool sites about subjects that are somewhat tenuously related to the material in the book. You might not learn much from these, but you'll have fun poking around.

By the way, this whole chapter is being reproduced in e-mail format on my website, **www.screamingcapitalist.com/ bookresources**. This will save you the trouble of keying all this stuff in and will allow you to stay connected if any of the links listed here break. The site also includes a form for submitting suggestions on other websites we can add to the list. If the site makes the cut, you'll receive all the credit and glory.

Introduction
Websites
www.80s.com/cgi-bin/80smain.cgi
Features a piece called "Children of the Eighties." If you're still not sure if this book is for you, read this. If you can relate, it is.

www.coupland.com
This is Douglas Coupland's official website. In case you're not familiar with the name, Coupland is the author of *Generation X* and *Girlfriend in a Coma*, among other things. He's like the official spokesperson of your generation, so check this site out. It's so cool that I have no idea what it is about!

www.netwalk.com/~duchapl/
The baby boomers' home page. A good way to scope out the competition.

Chapter 1
Websites
206.75.36.123/services_public/serv_pub.html
The address should give you a hint. Despite appearances to the contrary, this is the chartered accountants' official site. Not the most exciting page, but, hey, they're accountants!

www.caifa.com/informed_consumer/inf_consumer_body.
html
The official site of the Canadian Association of Insurance and Financial
Advisors. This particular address will take you to their section on finding
the right advisor.

www.cba.org
The Information Service of the Canadian Bar Association. Click on
"Sections" and then go to the area you need help with. Lots of good basic
information, but pretty dry reading.

www.cga-canada.org/eng/designation/profiles.htm
A touching, in-depth portrayal of a life lived as a Chartered General
Accountant—the debits, the credits. . . . How can you possibly resist read-
ing this right away?

www.gettingadvice.ca/
Operated by Fidelity Investments, this is an excellent site on finding a
financial advisor. In addition to providing information on building your
relationship, the site lets you download information booklets in PDF or
order them—free.

www.investorlearning.ca/ilcdev/
The Investor Learning Centre has excellent information on investing and
how to choose a stockbroker.

www.lawsocietyalberta.com/public_legal/default.asp
This site will give you a good basic understanding of the process of going
to a lawyer: What is needed, what is expected and what you can reasonably ask for. It features a sample lawyer FAQ page—and if you don't know
what a FAQ is, I'm not sure you're under 35.

Chapter 2
Websites
www.cibc.com/english/personal_services/borrowing/credit_cards/qu
ick_compare.html
The CIBC Card Comparer. A good example of the type of credit card site
all the banks offer.

www.equifax.ca/EFX_Canada/consumer_information_centre/overview_e
.html
One of the best sites in Canada on consumer credit. Get some popcorn
and read through the FAQ section.

www.frugal-moms.com/
This site uses forums and articles to demonstrate that "being frugal is not about being stingy—it's about being smart with your money so you can afford the things that are really important to you."

www.life.ca/subject/simplicity.html
The "Voluntary Simplicity" site. Although some might consider this an anti-financial site (it's run by *Natural Life* magazine and is fairly "green"), I figure that part of financial planning is helping clients quantify and then achieve their goals. Essays like the ones posted on this site may help us discern what is truly important to us.

www.simpleliving.net
For the hardcore "change your life, don't fret the money and hug a tree" crowd.

Books
The Millionaire Next Door: The Surprising Secrets of America's Wealthy, by Thomas J. Stanley and William D. Danko, Pocket Books, 2000.

Your Money or Your Life, by Joe Dominguez and Vicki Robin, Penguin USA, 1999.

Chapter 3
Websites
www.theabsolutegroup.com
A very clever site, and the fellow who runs it is witty, tender-hearted and ruggedly handsome. He would certainly be a member of Mensa if they didn't have that tricky entrance exam, association fee and strict code of conduct. (If you haven't figured it out yet, this is *my* site!)

www.canoe.ca/MyMoney/index_tools.html
www.quicken.ca/eng/life/rrsp/how_much_calc/index.jsp
These two websites contain excellent Java-based calculators that can make planning for retirement or choosing an asset allocation (among other things) much easier. Just print the results and file them away.

Software
Quicken
MS Money
Excellent, multi-purpose financial planning software that allows you to create budgets and then generate reports showing how far "off" you are, plot the progress of your investments and even do your online banking

(downloading the transactions directly into the software). I use Quicken Deluxe, but have heard good things about MS Money.

Chapter 4
Websites
www.apa.ca/main.htm
The Automobile Protection Association's site. The APA provides an excellent service that will tell you what the dealer paid for the car that you're trying to buy, and will also link you with a dealership that will offer you that price plus a set fee, such as $1,000.

www.bizsmart.com/english/servlet/PreLogin
A banking service offered by Staples—the office supply store. Your small business account gets free chequing, interest and discounts on purchases.

www.canoe.ca/CNEWSGas/oil_oct8-cp.html
An article about how car-sharing works.

www.carinsurance.ca/informationindex.asp
Good basic information on car insurance, including some quick quotes.

www.citizensbank.ca/insidecitizens/different.html
The online banking arm of VanCity Credit Union, the Citizens Bank offers an alternative to regular banks.

www.cmhc-schl.gc.ca/
The Canada Mortgage and Housing Corporation's site offers all sorts of information about mortgages and the home-buying process. They will also send you a great booklet called *A Consumer Guide to Buying a Home*.

www.cooperativeauto.net
The website of one of the car-sharing organizations.

www.gov.mb.ca/agriculture/homeec/cba28s01.html
This is the branch of the Manitoba government that tracks the costs of raising a child. They put out an excellent summary of this information every year.

www.ingdirect.ca/www/howdoesitwork.jsp
ING Direct uses the Internet to provide high-interest savings accounts, term deposits and alternative loans.

www.orea.com/consumer/default.asp
The consumer area of the Ontario Real Estate Association's website provides basic information on buying and selling a house.

www.tdcanadatrust.com/mortgages/
Lots of fundamental information on mortgages. The site includes an excellent mortgage calculator that will help you determine the savings you'd realize if you paid your mortgage off quickly. It also helps you strategize how best to do this.

Books

Don't Get Taken Every Time, by Remar Sutton, Penguin, 2001.

How to Buy Your Home, by the Ontario Real Estate Association, 1999. Order free by calling 1-800-563-4663.

Chapter 5
Websites

Most of the sites listed here offer an e-mail service that is very handy when it comes to keeping up to date with changes.

www.fundlibrary.com
Since I am the managing editor of this site, I will disclose my bias: Fundlibrary.com is the best mutual fund aggregation site in the country. There, I've said it!
—Stephen Kangas
The Fund Library is unique because it provides an aggregation of all mutual fund ratings in one easy-to-use filter tool. It includes the Morningstar, Globefund, Fundata and Gordon Pape ratings. In addition, it consolidates the ratings into a single composite score out of 100. It also includes a plethora of content from financial advisors and investment professionals, return information and statistics, and an e-mail service that keeps you informed about anything (a fund, a firm, a particular topic) that you wish to track.

www.Globefund.com
This site features some *Globe and Mail* content and indexes all of the paper's articles by fund company. It includes a proprietary five-star rating system, as well as lots of return information, charts, statistics and a great portfolio tracker. Users can sign up for an e-mail service to receive updates.

www.globeinvestor.com/
The stock market site from the *Globe and Mail*, complete with a simple stock list, filters and a portfolio service.

money.msn.ca/
Part of the monster MSN conglomerate, this site has some original financial content I find useful.

www.Morningstar.ca
The Morningstar site features its own five-star rating system; content provided by a stable of mutual fund writers like Gordon Powers and Rudy Luukko; lots of return information and statistics; and an e-mail summary of recent articles.

www.nationalpost.com
The best thing about the *National Post* website is that they store articles here for up to 60 days, making it possible to find material from papers that are weeks old. They also have a free daily e-mail that sends out the headlines.

www.quicken.ca/
This site borrows heavily from the even larger **quicken.com** (its American big brother), but provides information that's directly applicable to Canadians. Comes complete with calculators, portfolios and real-time quotes.

Books
Beating the Street, by Peter Lynch, Distican Incorporated, 1994.

Fund Monitor 2000, by Duff Young, Prentice Hall Canada, 1999.

Top Funds 2001: Building Your Mutual Fund Portfolio for the 21st Century, by Nick Fallor, Riley Moynes, Prentice Hall Canada, 2000.

The Warren Buffet Way, by Robert G. Hagstrom, Jr., John Wiley & Sons, 1994.

Chapter 6
Websites
CCRA help sites:

www.ccra-adrc.gc.ca/E/pub/tg/t4040eq/t4040-e.pdf
PDF guide on RRSPs, RPPs and RRIFs.

www.fin.gc.ca/budget98/pamphe/edupae.html
PDF guide on the CESG for RESPs.

www.ccra-adrc.gc.ca/E/pub/tg/rc4112eq/rc4112-e.pdf

PDF guide on the lifelong learning program.

Chapter 7
Websites
www.ccra-adrc.gc.ca/menu-e.html
The Canada Customs and Revenue Agency site is relatively painless to use. The search engine makes up for the drab layout and somewhat disorganized format. The site essentially stores all of the budgets, tax forms, interpretation bulletins and booklets (in PDF format) you will ever need.

www.kpmg.ca/english/services/tax/
An excellent example of one of the big six accounting firms' sites, complete with headlines, tax tips and summarized strategies. Like any commercial site, it is designed to lure you into the nearest KPMG office—but the no-cost, hassle-free information available here is worth delving into.

www.waterstreet.ca/
This is Tim Cestnick's website. For those of you who may not be aware, Cestnick is the world-famous (well, in Canada, anyway) accountant who writes for *The Globe and Mail* and other publications. He has a couple of books and also tours the country opening for Marilyn Manson... I think. If accountants are too funny, their own associations make them pay fines. All of Tim's *Globe and Mail* articles are collected here and there is an excellent tax discussion forum as well.

Books
201 Easy Ways to Reduce Your Taxes, by Evelyn Jacks, McGraw-Hill Ryerson, 1999.

Jacks on Tax Savings: 2001, by Evelyn Jacks, McGraw-Hill Ryerson, 2000.

Winning the Tax Game 2002, by Tim Cestnick, Prentice Hall Canada, 2001.

Chapter 8
Websites
www.ca-probate.com/wills.htm
A site that publishes the wills of celebrities and ordinary people (1493–1998). A little wacky, but fun if you're into that stuff.

www.harbour.sfu.ca/gero/pubs/pensbook.html
This site offers a beginner's guide to Canada's public pension system and includes a great explanation and exploration of the CPP, OAS, etc.

www.life-line.org/life/index.html
The Life-line site offers basic insurance information and an excellent INA (that's industry jargon for insurance needs analysis) calculator. It's also full of warm, cuddly photos of extraordinarily good-looking, well-adjusted and well-insured people.

www.quicken.ca/eng/life/rrsp/insurance/showcontent.jsp?cid=100357
A good summary of disability insurance issues from quicken.ca.

www.take-a-wiz.com/default.asp
This is actually an estate planning site. Trust me. It is filled with "wizards" to help you complete your estate planning needs, locate your important documents, etc.

Glossary

amortization period
The period over which a mortgage is amortized. (Duh!) This is often 15, 20 or 25 years. See *amortize*.

amortize
To liquidate or reduce a debt by regular payments into a sinking fund.

annuity
A contract or agreement to receive fixed payments on an investment over a set time frame (for life or a set number of years). From the Latin *annus* (see *arrears* and *asset*).

arrears
Slang: more than one rear. Seriously, see Chapter 2, I defined it there.

asset
A really nice arrear. (Kidding.)

asset class
A type of investment such as a stock or bond.

attribution rules
If you do not do it properly, the CCRA will thwart your attempt to "split income" with your family. For example, if you gift $175,000 to your five-year-old son so that he can buy a rental property and then try to claim that rental income as his, the CCRA (after chuckling in it's evil way), will "attribute" the income back to you.

audit
I have no idea really, but it sounds bad. Avoid one of these.

bank
?...This one is a bank...a *bank*...you know, right?

blue chip stock
Blue Chip stocks are stocks issued by the largest, most stable companies. Supposedly, the term "blue chip" refers to the fact that, in gambling, blue chips have one of the highest values.

boomer
Aussie slang for kangaroo; Canadian slang for anyone born between the 1946 and 1964, roughly.

Canada Pension Plan (CPP)
Old Age Security (OAS)
Guaranteed Income Supplement (GIS)
Ogo-Pogo
Myths; forget about them.

Canada Savings Bond (CSB)
Almost useless for anything except short term saving. Like a cashable GIC or term deposit from the bank with a lower rate and a funkier television commercial.

capital gain
A gain on your capital. You buy comic books at, say, two for a nickel because some poor misunderstood kid was forced to sell it by his mother (who didn't ever really understand him). You later sell one of those comics for $750. The difference between purchase price and selling price is your capital gain.

capital loss
A loss on your capital. You buy some vintage "If this van's a rockin' don't come a knockin'" bumper stickers for $55 dollars and sell them later at a garage sale for $0.25. That's a loss of your capital.

capitalist
Opposite of a Commie-Pinko.

CCRA
Canada Customs and Revenue Agency, formerly Revenue Canada. Different name, same great taste!

collateral
Some security to guarantee a loan. With a mortgage, for example, the house is the collateral. This term is also used in action films to describe the kind of damage where everyone in the elite platoon *except* the hero gets killed.

credit card interest
When you want to have a credit card, you express interest.

debenture
An unsecured loan; a loan without collateral. Like a government bond (I just threw this one in here to show off).

deficit
This is what happens when you spend *more* than you make.

devalued dollar
Future dollars; dollars that have been eroded in value because of inflation. In 1930, $1 would have bought roughly what $43 today would buy. (Okay, I just made up that number, but you get what I mean, right?)

echo boom
A mini "boomlet" of kids born to the Baby Boomers.

elimination period
The period between when you first getting sick or disabled and when the disability insurance payment kicks in. Probably called "elimination" because it is the time when you have to eliminate a lot of things—like luxury vehicles, sports equipment, meals, etc., to pay for your disability.

emergency fund
A small pot of cash set aside for emergencies, such as the release of the *Godfather* trilogy DVDs.

equity
Ownership, typically in stocks.

facecrime
From George Orwell's lovely, happy book, *1984*. Orwell's definition; "*It was terribly dangerous to let your thoughts wander when you were in any public place or within range of a telescreen. The smallest thing could give you away. A nervous tic, an unconscious look of anxiety, a habit of muttering to yourself—anything that carried with it the suggestion of abnormality, of having something to hide. In any case, to wear an improper expression on your face (to look incredulous when a victory was announced, for example) was itself a punishable offence.*
There was even a word for it in Newspeak: facecrime, it was called." (This worries me because I mutter to myself... no you don't... yes I DO... what does this definition have to do with money?... QUIET!)

fund performance
An analysis of how well a particular mutual fund performed. This is supposed to be determined over years of comparative analysis but is usually determined by either looking at the Top/Bottom Performers for the Month or by reading mutual fund company ads in the business section of the paper.

Gen-Xer
Those currently 25 to 35 years old, roughly. Between the Boomers and the Echo Boomers. Think *Friends* with smaller apartments and not as good looking.

GIC

Guaranteed Investment
Certificate. Available from
banks and trusts companies,
with a similar product also
available from life insurance
companies. GICs are popular
with Canadians looking for a
simple investment that offers
three concrete guarantees:

1. The principal
2. The interest rate
3. The gradual erosion of your
   money once taxes and inflation eat it away

gross income

This is not a reflection of the low
wage you make. It is merely your
income before taxes are
deducted.

index (indices)

A measure of a certain stock
market, calculated from some of
its major company stocks.
Examples: TSE300 (a collection
of 300 stocks that represent the
stocks on the Toronto Stock
Exchange), MSCI World (an
index put out by Morgan Stanley
Capital International that covers
the world's major markets).

ITF (in trust for) account

A simple account set up for by
an adult "in trust for" a minor.
This is because most banks, trust
and mutual fund companies will
not create an account for anyone
under the age of majority since

children cannot legally enter into
or be bound by legal contracts.
The ITF is not an official CCRA-
recognized trust, it is merely an
administrative convention.

inflation

The gradual and perpetual erosion of the purchasing power
of the dollar. On May 24, 1626,
Peter Minuit supposedly bought
Manhattan Island from the
natives for $24 of beads. These
days, that same $24 will not even
let you buy a single bead when
you're in Manhattan.

intestate

Dying without a will—which led
to the term "testy" as a descrip-
tion of your heirs attitudes when
having to deal with fall-out.

liquidity

A term to describe how "cashable" an investment is, i.e., how
quickly it can be turned into
spendable moola.

Love Jar, The

(pronounced "Luvvvvv JAR-
RRRR" in a Rasta kind of way ...)
We keep a small clay pot near the
bed and use it to collect spare
change. The amount we put into
the pot is fixed, the times we
"deposit" are not. Sometimes I
put money into this pot, other
times my wife does ... sometimes we *both* put money in. I
deposit a loonie each time while

my wife deposits a twoonie. She deposits dough less often than I do but puts double in so that our contributions equal out because I . . . make a deposit . . . almost twice as often as she does. She has repeatedly approached me about being able to . . . deposit money into the pot as often as I do but I thank her for her gracious offer and tell her it is not necessary. Sometimes we just don't have the time for *her* to make a deposit and . . . anyway, get it?

management expense ratio (MER)

This is a percentage calculating the costs of running a mutual fund. This is assumed by some to affect the long term performance of a mutual fund. (See my next book for a detailed discussion of this . . . assuming there *is* a next book.)

mutual funds license

A license, issued by provincial Securities Commissions, to offer open ended mutual funds to the public.

net return

The amount of return you have left after all costs, expenses and usually taxes and inflation are calculated. For example, if you have an investment that earned 10% the gross return is 10%. The net return would be 10%

less taxes of 30% (or 3% of the return) and then less inflation of 4%. This means the net return is 10% – 3% – 4% = 3%. 3%! So even though it SOUNDS "gross," it is actually net.

net worth

Your assets less your debts.

net worth statement

A piece of paper showing your assets less your debts.

old age security (OAS)

Sponging off your kids.

Prince Jefri of Brunei

The former Finance Minister, His Royal Highness Paduka Seri Pengiran Digadong Sahibul Mal Pengiran Muda Haji Jefri Bolkiah was caught embezzling money from the Sultan—his very own brother! Before that rough family time, he was a rocker of a capitalist. He owned hotels and banks and even a huge yacht named *Tits* with two smaller tender craft called *Nipple 1* and *Nipple 2*. You *gotta* love that. Alas, now that he is in disgrace, the courts have heartlessly cut back his spending allowance to just $300,000 a month! How can he properly support his wives that way?

principal

This is the money you put into an investment; the original capital.

quartile
When mutual funds are ranked on their performance, they are divided into quarters or quartiles. A first quartile fund has performed among the top 25% of all similar funds for that time frame. This is an apples-to-apples comparison, not an absolute measurement so a fund that has a -67% return can still brag about being a top quartile performer!

spousal RRSP
An RRSP you buy for your spouse where the money grows in their name while you get the initial income tax benefit.

stock market
A place you go to buy a partnership (or stock) in some business.

stock market crash
This is reported when some stock market index drops a lot. You will see headlines about the market "PLUNGING 1.6%" one day, looming global depression the next, and the "remarkable soaring recovery" the day after that.

term deposit
See GIC

The Six Steps
A famous film by Alfred Hitchcock where he plots out the bone-chilling suspense of generating a financial plan!

treasury bill
This is like a GIC issued by the government. Often used by the banks to fund savings accounts and make massive profits.

volatility
HUGE DROPS! KILLED! SLAMMED! "CHEWED UP!" "THUMPED!"
(But really just large swings in value. People forget volatile also means large *upward* swings in value.)

will
1. free; 2. opposite of "won't" and the perfect rebuttal in that most simple of all arguments (except the even more classic "am not/am so"); 3. a legal declaration of how a person wants his stuff divided up when he is dead.

Index